map your
FINANCIAL FUTURE
starting the right path
in your teens and twenties

To Kiera,
I hope you enjoy the book. May God bless you.

PATRICK A. LYONS

Copyright © 2006 by Patrick Lyons

First Edition

This publication is designed to provide competent and reliable information regarding the subject matter covered. However, it is sold with the understanding that the author and publisher are not engaged in rendering legal, financial or other professional advice. Law practices vary from state to state. If legal or other expert assistance is required, consult the services of a professional should be sought. The author and publisher specifically disclaim any liability that is incurred from the use or application of the contents of this book.

While the author has made every effort to provide accurate telephone numbers and Internet addresses at the time of publication, neither the publisher nor author assumes any responsibility for errors or for changes that occur after publication.

All rights reserved. No part of this document may be reproduced or transmitted in any form or by any means, electronic, mechanical, photocopying, recording, or otherwise, without prior written permission of Lyons Den Press.

Quantity discounts available. Contact the publisher at the address below for details:

Lyons Den Press
P.O. Box 1341
Durham, North Carolina 27702
www.PatrickALyons.com

ISBN: 978-1-4116-8677-9

Printed in the United States of America

*To my wife Kelly and daughter Jordan
Thank you for all of your love, support
and inspiration.*

*In Memory of my Dad
Charlie James Lyons
Thank you for all the life lessons
you taught.*

acknowledgments

First, and foremost, I want to thank you, the reader, for your support. I am honored that you have chosen to buy my book and hope that after reading, you will add it to your personal library and will refer to it often as you tackle the financial challenges of life.

Kelly Starling Lyons, my wife, thank you for being a sounding board for my ideas and for giving so much. You shared your journalistic expertise, offered constructive criticism and pushed me to complete this project. I could not have done this book without you. I love you.

To my daughter, Jordan Gabrielle Lyons, thank you for loving me and making me take breaks from writing to appreciate the precious jewel that you are. You will always be "Daddy's little girl."

To my mom, Gwendolyn Arline Lyons, one of my biggest supporters, I will never be able to repay you for all you have given me. Thank you for your love and for keeping me grounded.

To my dad, Charlie James Lyons, who passed away before this book was finished, thank you for the wisdom you imparted so freely. I miss all of the stories you used to share.

To my big brother, Charlie James Lyons, Jr., thanks for being the best brother anyone could ask for. You are one of the smartest people I know and I don't think I could ever explain how much you mean to me.

To my grandmother, affectionately known as Mur, you are in better shape than all seven of your children and most of your grandchildren. You are one of the strongest women I know. You're an inspiration.

To Maceo K. Sloan, thank you for taking a chance on me 11 years ago and giving me my first job in the investment industry. I appreciate your support of this book. I enjoy the working relationship we have and appreciate all of the advice (professional and personal) you have shared over the years.

acknowledgments, cont'd

To Diallo Johnson, a great friend, your stories inspired parts of this book. It's amazing how much we have grown since our college days. In this cutthroat world of business, it's nice knowing I can depend on a friend like you for support.

To Wendell Mackey, who was like my brother away from home when I started working in the investment industry, thank you for taking me under your wing and showing me the ropes.

To Craig Reed, thank you for sharing your stories of young people with financial problems. They helped inspire me to write this book.

I'd also like to acknowledge the hard work of people behind the scenes. This book would not have come together without them. Thanks to my copy editors, Debra Boyette and Catherine Van Herrin, for doing an outstanding job. Thanks to Tracy Carr who designed the creative interior layout. Thanks to Amie Brooks for the eye-catching cover. Many thanks to my publicist, Edrea Davis, for her diligence in helping me promote this book. Thanks to Smitha Poluri for a creative website.

To all of my reviewers, Chris Duhon, Vivian Harper, Denise Barton, Beauford Hicks, Vicky Armstrong, Lois Center-Shabazz, Chris Surrey, Darrell Luzzo, Richard Smith, Landon Adams, Antoine Medley, Donald Barringer, Taurean Blacque, Gina Dean, Tom Kerr, Patricia Hackenschmidt, Sarah Combs, Charles Dino and Debra Austin, thank you for your feedback. I owe a special thank you to Maxine Sweet of Experian, Roberta Boyd-Norfleet of Self-Help Credit Union and Susan Lupton of Center for Responsible Lending for their technical review of the manuscript.

There are many others who mean so much to me – and supported me in countless ways. Although you are not mentioned by name, know that you are remembered in my heart.

Praise for *Map Your Financial Future*

Chris Duhon
Guard, Chicago Bulls
Map Your Future presents information on budgeting, managing credit and saving for the future in an easy to understand language making this a must read for anyone starting out of his or her own.

Richard A. Smith
Regional Director, INROADS Florida Region
Map Your Financial Future hits the heart of the financial information our kids need as they begin their careers.

Darrell Luzzo, Ph.D.
Senior Vice President – Education, Junior Achievement Worldwide
Mr. Lyons has done a FANTASTIC job with this book. His writing style is engaging and easy to follow, and at the same time he addresses several concepts that are central to the success of youth as they manage their finances. Congratulations on a job very, very well done!

Lois Center-Shabazz,
Author "Let's Get Financial Savvy"! Founder of the personal finance website, www.Msfinancialsavvy.com
Map Your Future is an attention grabbing, easy to use, step-by-step solutions book. The author speaks in a tone that the average 16-29 year old can clearly understand and relate to the topic of money and spending it. Understanding financial woes from banking to bankruptcy in *Map Your Future* will save many a young soul.

Roberta Boyd-Norfleet
Regional Branch Director, Central Branch/Durham, Self-Help Credit Union
Patrick did his homework on things to consider when deciding whether to rent or buy a house. His information on things to consider when choosing a mortgage is on point.

Beauford Hicks
Superintendent, Mitchell County Georgia School System
This book will help you manage your money more effectively and make wiser financial decisions. This is one you must own.

Craig Reed
Director of Health & Fitness, Marine Corps Community Service, Camp Lejeune

Praise for *Map Your Financial Future*, cont'd.

I encounter so many young people on a daily basis with credit trouble and am glad Patrick talks about what you can do to get back on track if you become overwhelmed with credit and plan for your retirement.

Diallo Johnson
Senior Vice President, Director of Research – FIS Group
I wish this book were around when I was growing up. Young adults should buy this book, read it and keep it as a reference for many years.

Keith and Belinda Shannon
Founders, Preparing America's Tomorrow Today
If you want a book that presents real world advice on personal finance issues in practical terms then this is the book for you.

Wendell Mackey
Principal – Director of Investments, Channing Capital Management, LLC
This book provides solid information that will not only help young adults get their financial house in order, it will help the more mature crowd reset their direction as well.

Taurean Blacque
Actor
Mr. Lyons addresses financial issues that many young adults will encounter and provides recommendations on triumphing over major obstacles like credit trouble and identity theft. Following the advice presented in this book will lead you to financial freedom.

Vicky Armstrong
Student, Meredith College
The fact that Patrick presents examples of places that teens and twenty-something's frequent is great. Seeing illustrations of shopping for shoes or going out to a fast food place like McDonald's or a coffee shop like Starbucks made it seem more relevant to my life as a college student. I really think *Map Your Future* will be a huge help to people my age to get things in order for the real world as well as a means to introduce high school kids to real world practices.

Antoine Medley
Executive Director/Founder, Future Black Men of America, Inc
This book is very easy to read and understand filled with practical tips to help you achieve financial freedom.

table of contents

Introduction 1

Part 1 – Tools for the Journey **7**

Chapter 1 – Budgeting 9

Chapter 2 – Comparing Banks and Credit Unions 23

Part 2 – On-the-Road Experience **33**

Chapter 3 – Understanding Credit 35

Chapter 4 – Breaking Down Credit Reports 53

Chapter 5 – Navigating Credit Problems 63

Chapter 6 – Avoiding Identity Theft 73

Part 3 – The Pit Stop **85**

Chapter 7 – Defining Financial Freedom 87

Chapter 8 – Starting a Business 99

table of contents, cont'd

Part 4 — In the Homestretch **111**

Chapter 9 – Education Never Ends 113

Chapter 10 – Renting and Buying 123

Chapter 11 – Investment Basics 141

Chapter 12 – Retirement Planning 161

Epilogue 177

About the Author 179

Resources 181

Index 193

foreword

When Patrick Lyons asked me to write the foreword to his book, I was honored because it is so timely and needed. In my 30-plus years in the investment industry, I've met my share of people who struggled to get control of their finances. As I reflect on the important advice offered in these pages, I wish others could have read Patrick's words when they were young.

You hold in your hands a plan for financial success. Whether you are just learning about money management or have been figuring it out as you go along, *Map Your Financial Future* can help you claim victory. Patrick graciously taps more than a decade of experience to show you how to grow wealth, avoid and bounce back from money troubles and find financial freedom. He shares advice, information and life lessons in a way that's easy to understand and apply.

Each chapter presents the fundamentals of areas such as budgeting, credit and investing while speaking to the concerns of your generation.

In today's world of bankruptcies and credit difficulties, this book gives hope of turning things around. The future of a nation rests in its young people. If you take Patrick's challenge and learn the ins-and-outs of finances, you can be leaders of a new era.

Map Your Financial Future is essential for anyone wishing to get off to the right start. If you heed its message, you will be on the road to a bright future.

Maceo K. Sloan, CFA, FLMI
Chairman, CEO and CIO
NCM Capital

INTRODUCTION

≫ The Journey Begins

The path to financial freedom starts by recognizing it takes hard work and time to reach your goals.

Planning for the future is a journey. Some paths lead to success and others run into roadblocks. Without a map, it's easy to get off track. You can be cruising one moment and hit a dead-end or take a turn that makes you lose your direction. On every voyage, you need something to guide you. This book will help direct your way.

The first rule of the road is making good choices. Decisions we make today impact our financial future. Peer pressure can cause us to spend our money frivolously. Patterns learned from parents influence our decisions. Then, we have our own desires. How many times have you walked into a department store and planned to just browse, but ended up buying something? We've all been there. But next time, ask yourself: How will this purchase affect me in the future?

To get on the right path financially, it is important to distinguish between wants and needs. It's ok to buy items you want, but realize there may be consequences. Consider an impulse buy of $200 jeans. That splurge may mean not having the funds for unexpected car repairs or using a credit card for purchases because you're short on cash. That means taking out a loan that has to be repaid.

For young adults living on your own, the money choices you make today can shape your future. If you are doing a good job managing your finances, you probably have some money left after you pay the bills. If you are living beyond your means, you may not have the money you need when it counts.

For young people in high school or college, independence can feel like a long time away. But before you know it, you will be on your own to tackle all of the challenges - including the financial ones - of being an adult. That transition will be a lot easier if you develop the skills to manage money wisely.

Personal finance may be something you've never considered. Schools teach a lot of useful subjects, but money management is rarely covered. A lot of what we learn about money comes from popular culture and our parents.

Television and movies show the glamour of spending, but not the sweat required to earn – and grow — the money that lifestyle requires. Some young adults see mom or dad maxing out credit cards or missing payments. Often, we miss the stories of people overwhelmed by debt who lose their homes and sink into depression. The goal of this book is to give you a strong foundation to help make your financial ride through life a smooth one.

MY STORY

I fell into the credit card trap when I was in high school. Senior year brought lots of bills — pictures, school trips, the prom, class ring. Add the expense of clothing and gas for my car and I was over my head. Although I had a part-time job, it never seemed enough to meet the demands on my limited funds. I didn't want to be a burden on my parents, so I started applying for credit.

The first card I received was from Sears. I was given a $500 limit. Next, I went to my credit union and took out a $300 loan to buy a class ring and help with other senior expenses. I paid the loan off on time, but started struggling to keep up with payments on my Sears card. College was coming so I bought items for my future apartment and some new clothes. By this time, my credit limit had risen from $500 to $1,000. It wasn't long before I maxed out my new limit too. I didn't have the money to pay the bill.

Four years later, I had accumulated more than $6,000 in debt from two credit cards, and $8,000 from student loans, and I had no job to pay it off. I felt crushed under the weight of my bills.

In 1995, a year after graduation, I took charge of my financial life. My first job paid $23,000 a year. I decided to find a way to live off my income. I came up with a plan to pay off my debts one by one. I started with the small bills. As I got raises, I paid more on my debts. I kept track of my expenses and put myself on a budget. It took six years to erase those outstanding balances completely. The day I paid off my last bill was a time of celebration. I vowed never to get in that situation again.

PRIDE

Pride gets a bad rap sometimes. But it can be a pathway to success. I have turned the word PRIDE into an acronym for a formula to win in life:

"P" stands for **Preparation**. Good fortune is hardly ever the result of luck. To be successful in any endeavor requires hard work.

"R" stands for **Respect**. Honor yourself and elders. I went through a phase where I thought I knew everything. Our parents, grandparents and others have knowledge that we should take advantage of. They have gone through many of life's challenges we have yet to face.

"I" stands for **Individualism.** Leaders never follow the crowd. They stand out because they have vision and are willing to take risks.

"D" stands for **Discipline**. Once you have a plan, stay the course no matter how tough things become. Life rarely goes as planned. We can succeed by being patient, believing in ourselves and moving forward with our goals.

If you can live by the principles of **Preparation**, **Respect**, **Individualism** and **Discipline**, you will **Excel** in life, which is what the **"E"** stands for.

HOW DO YOU USE THIS BOOK?

Map Your Financial Future is divided into four sections to steer you on your journey. Part One lays out the tools for the journey by covering budgeting and money-saving tips to assist in reaching your goals. Part Two explores how to effectively navigate the bumpy path of credit so it doesn't become a road block. Part Three discusses moves you can take to increase your earnings potential. Part Four talks about ways to build your nest egg for retirement.

Chapters, filled with tips, definitions and worksheets, make up each section. At the end of each chapter, you'll find the summary, "Shortcuts," which goes over the most important topics. If you're a teen, look for "Just for Teens," a special box with tips written just for you.

Charting your financial future in your teens and twenties gives you a head start. It doesn't matter if you're just entering the real world and starting to establish bank and credit accounts or if you're working and made some financial mistakes.

If you follow the principles in this book, you will reach your destination of financial independence in no time.

PART 1

≫ Tools for the Journey

CHAPTER 1

≫ Budgeting

Discipline is required to follow a budget. But it has wiggle room too. You balance wants and needs to maximize your income.

Developing a budget represents the "P" (Preparation) and "D" (Discipline) in PRIDE. A budget is a plan that helps guide you in reaching your financial goals. Think of it as a compass. When you veer off track with spending, you can pull it out to find your way.

If you discover that your initial plan is too restrictive, adjust it. Having a budget means making choices. Maybe you pick one party to attend instead of going out every night of the week. Maybe you still treat yourself to new shoes, but you look for a sale instead of paying full price.

Setting up a Budget

A budget provides an estimate of the money coming in and the money paid out in expenses. It is designed to help you see where your money is going and keep you from spending more than you bring home.

I set my first budget by making a list of all of my costs and tracking them in a spreadsheet. After monitoring these expenses for a couple of months, I could see how much my bills were and make good estimates of what they would be in the future. With that information, I gave myself an allowance. This was spending money I could use for things I wanted to buy after my bills were paid. Once I spent my allowance, that was it. I had to wait until my next paycheck before receiving more pocket money. I learned to make it stretch.

It's important to reward yourself for meeting financial goals. So as I paid off a debt or got a raise, I gave myself a slight boost in my allowance. I used that money to buy whatever I wanted. A budget is not punishment. You can make room for fun and still plan for the future.

A worksheet at the end of this chapter will help you construct a budget. List all of your expenses. If you go to Starbucks to get a latte in the morning or go by McDonald's to get a combo meal for lunch, create a category in your budget for dining out and record those costs on the form. This exercise will help you find areas to trim. Rent/mortgage payments tend to be the largest expense category for most people. If after cutting back on smaller expenses, you find you don't have enough income to pay your bills, consider finding a cheaper place to live or getting a roommate to share the bills. As a rule of thumb, mortgage/rent payment should not exceed 32% of your gross income. So if you are making $2,000 a month before taxes, your rent or mortgage payment should be no more than $640 per month.

I found that keeping a record of my bills and purchases made me think twice before charging something I could not afford.

Sample Expense Worksheet

Date	Store	Item	Cost
3-Aug	American Eagle	Jeans	$198
4-Aug	McDonalds	Big Mac Combo	$5
7-Aug	Shell	Gas	$25
15-Aug	Foot Locker	Shoes	$80
17-Aug	Starbucks	Hot Cocoa	$3
19-Aug	Applebee's	Hamburger	$8
19-Aug	Baskin-Robbins	Ice Cream	$4
21-Aug	Jaluka Juice	Smoothie	$5
23-Aug	Raines High School	2 Football tickets	$10
23-Aug	Limelight	Party	$20
24-Aug	The Moon	Party	$20

Monthly Total $378

Sample Monthly Budget

	Budget Amount	Actual Amount	Budget - Actual
INCOME			
Paycheck	$2,000.00	$2,000.00	$0.00
Business Income	$0.00	$0.00	$0.00
Total Income	$2,000.00	$2,000.00	$0.00
EXPENSES			
Car payment	$250.00	$250.00	$0.00
Rent	$560.00	$560.00	$0.00
Car Insurance	$70.00	$70.00	$0.00
Groceries	$100.00	$120.00	($20.00)
Cell Phone	$50.00	$75.00	($25.00)
Utilities	$120.00	$130.00	($10.00)
Entertainment	$200.00	$300.00	($100.00)
Credit card	$100.00	$120.00	($20.00)
Donations - Church	$200.00	$200.00	$0.00
Savings	$100.00	$175.00	($75.00)
Total Expenses	$1,750.00	$2,000.00	($250.00)
Income minus expenses	$250.00	$0.00	$0.00

Personal Finance Software Programs

In 1997, I started using Microsoft Money computer software to keep track of my finances. If you are computer savvy, I would recommend using a personal finance package such as Money or Quicken. These programs can help you set a budget, establish a retirement savings plan, set up a debt reduction strategy and balance your checkbook.

Microsoft Money can take the financial information you've entered and generate reports showing where your money is going. One time, the program made a note that my dining-out expenses jumped from 5% of my monthly expenses to 12%. This caused me to start bringing my lunch from home again. I also tried to find more reasonably-priced restaurants when I ate out for lunch and dinner.

After about six months of using Money, I realized that I exceeded my budget several times. I had to determine whether my budget needed adjusting or my spending habits. Here's a clue to figuring out which one to fix: If your income is the same, but expenses are growing then spending needs to be reduced. If you have some leeway after bills are paid and find your current plan is too rigid, it's OK to increase your budget.

Another reason to modify your budget is if some of your monthly recurring bills, like car insurance, rent and utilities, have increased. If you don't want to change your plan, shop around for better deals. Every dollar spent on essential bills is one dollar less for the things you want to do. When income equals expenses, it is called a balanced budget.

The ease of acquiring credit cards has allowed many people to spend more even when their income and savings aren't enough to buy the things they want. But when expenses exceed income, we are in a deficit. Stated another way, we are living beyond our means. If the problem is allowed to worsen, it can turn into a disaster and lead to bankruptcy.

According to the Administrative Office of U.S. Courts, more than 1.6 million people filed for bankruptcy in fiscal 2004. Bankruptcy occurs when you have more expenses than income and decide to petition the Federal Courts for either reorganization or liquidation. It should be a last resort. Reorganization means the government will come up with a plan to lower payments on your debts so you can still pay them off. Liquidation means your obligation to pay your debts is essentially wiped away. In either case, the consequences are bad because a bankruptcy filing remains on your credit report for 10 years. (See chapters four and five for more information on credit reports and bankruptcy.)

Emergency Fund

Unexpected expenses are a fact of life. Let's say you get laid off from your job. With the loss of your job comes the loss of your health insurance. What do you do if you have a medical emergency or need prescription medications while you are out of work? Then, there are unexpected car and home repairs. In these and other circumstances, credit cards and loans can be a source of taking care of bills. But there's another option: Establish an emergency fund before the problems occur.

Setting up an emergency fund can reduce the need to use credit when you're in a bind. Instead of reaching for your charge card, you just withdraw money from the account you've reserved for these special circumstances. It's a good idea to work toward building a balance equal to four to six months of living expenses. The funds should be invested in a money market or savings account. These pay more in interest than a typical checking account. Money market accounts are also good because in cases of emergencies, you can get to the funds relatively quickly.

Four to six months of expenses may sound like a difficult goal. But you can get started by depositing a portion of each paycheck in this account. Start small and increase contributions as you're able. It will take some time to build your emergency fund, but you're moving in the right direction.

Splurge Fund

If you like to have spending sprees, one way to keep your budget under control is by setting up a splurge fund. Money in this account can be used on whatever you want. I suggest setting up a money market account or a savings account and determining your annual splurge budget. For instance, if you would like to reward yourself with $1,200 each year for special purchases or impulse buys, make monthly deposits of $100. Next, choose how often you would like to go on these shopping sprees and come up with a withdrawal schedule. Using the example above, if you want to do quarterly shopping sprees, you would have $300 every three months to spend as you wish ($1,200/4 = $300).

Money Saving Tips

Although you may not yet be making the income you wish, there are plenty of ways to stretch your dollars without sacrificing quality.

Clothing

Most Americans spend a lot of money on clothes. One way to save is to check out clearance racks. These clothes are in good shape but may be out of season so retailers lower prices to move them out the door. You can find good deals if you take the time to search.

Outlet malls are another source for bargains. They offer many name-brand items, but at lower prices than you can find at shopping malls. The clothes might be overstock or have slight imperfections that the mall stores could not sell.

Transportation

Between 2003 and 2005, oil prices doubled, driving gas prices higher as well. One way to shave transportation costs is to use regular unleaded gasoline instead of premium. Unless your vehicle specifically calls for premium gas, you could save 20 cents a gallon or more by using a lower grade of fuel. If a vehicle has a 14-gallon tank, the savings could be about $3 a week or approximately $150 per year. This savings could be applied to other expenses. Having tires properly inflated provides less road resistance and can help improve gas mileage. Taking it easy on the gas pedal can also save on fuel costs.

Another area to consider is the size of your vehicle. Some vendors charge more for scheduled maintenance on larger vehicles. Many sport utility vehicles are gas-guzzlers. In many cases, the longer the vehicle, the worse the gas mileage. Take the Ford Expedition, a large sport utility. It gets 14 miles per gallon in the city. The Ford Escape, a compact size sport utility, gets 20 to 22 miles per gallon in the city. The Ford Focus, a compact car, gets 26 miles per gallon in the city.

Switching from an Expedition to the Focus, could cut fuel costs by almost 50%.

Hybrid vehicles are another way to save on fuel costs. Hybrids use a combination of fuel and electricity to provide better gas mileage than conventional cars. Some hybrids, such as the Toyota Prius, deliver 60 miles per gallon in the city. Currently, hybrids cost more than comparable conventional vehicles, but prices are expected to drop as car manufacturers get more efficient at the manufacturing process.

Wholesale Clubs

Wholesale clubs such as BJ's, Costco and Sam's Club can be a great source for finding bargains on household items. These membership clubs usually require an annual fee to join. Some may also require that you work for a certain company or be a member of a particular organization. Clubs offer a variety of household items at prices lower than typical grocery and retail stores. These warehouses buy in bulk and are able to get favorable rates. They pass some of the savings on to their members.

Some of these clubs may require you to buy in large quantities to get the savings, but stores like Costco are offering its members the ability to buy in smaller amounts. If you are planning a party or cookout and need to buy in bulk, wholesale clubs can provide savings over grocery store prices. Also, some of these organizations offer discounts on products and services such as gas, car maintenance, eyeglasses and travel.

Online Shopping

Online shopping is becoming popular among consumers because companies typically offer lower prices than traditional stores. Expenses for Internet retailers are less than "bricks and mortar" stores because there are minimal overhead costs. Online retailers have warehouses with products, but they don't have to employ people to staff a traditional store.

You can find great deals online. When it comes to travel, Web sites like Expedia, Priceline and Travelocity offer discounts on airfare, hotel accommodations and rental cars. The major airlines and hotel chains also offer specials that are only available for online shoppers. Internet auction sites like eBay can offer savings compared to retail stores. I have made a habit of searching eBay before I buy certain items like electronic items or books. There is an old saying that "one man's trash is another man's treasure." I have found new and lightly-used products on eBay and saved more than 50% compared to retail prices. That's even counting shipping costs!

You can find great gift ideas for just about any occasion at online auctions for a fraction of the retail cost. While these sites can be a great way of saving, remember to be watchful for the danger of fraud. One way to lessen this risk is to look at a member's feedback rating before bidding on items. On eBay, I tend to only make bids on things from members who have a feedback rating of 98% or better and those who have done at least 50 transactions. That reassures me that particular member has done a fair amount of transactions and the majority of the customers were satisfied.

For buying from other online stores, consider using respected retailers like Wal-Mart and Target. Also check out Web sites such as Yahoo! or Shopping.com. These sites have standards that stores have to follow to be listed. Most retailers do not want to risk being kicked off a large Internet mall. They know it could hurt their sales and damage credibility among customers.

Finding a Roommate

If you are just starting out on your own, seeing your bills for the first time can be overwhelming. There's rent/mortgage, utilities (gas, electric, water), phone bill. On top of that, there are transportation costs (car payment and gas or public transportation), insurance (auto, life, renters/homeowners) and food to buy. Having a roommate can cut down on the sticker shock of living expenses.

If you choose to get a roommate, be sure to reach an agreement about how the bills will be split and when they will be paid. You may want to consider entering into a written contract. That way, both of you know the rules from the beginning. It can save a lot of frustration down the line.

NOTES

Just for Teens

As a high school student, many expenses come up during the school year. You can stay ahead of the crowd by developing a budget for major expenses. Here's a sample plan for the prom:

1 Start by listing all of your needs. Those could include transportation, tickets, formalwear, flowers. Develop your budget by coming up with an estimate for each expense. One way you can get an idea of costs is to talk to vendors. If you are looking for a dress, visit a few shops and take note of the price for styles you like. Come up with an average price. That will be your projected cost for that item. Repeat for each expense category.

2 Now you're ready to add everything up. Say your total is $400 for all expenses. That's your budget. Make sure your spending stays under that amount. If you need to tweak your budget along the way, that's fine. It may work out that you spend more on transportation, but less on food. Or maybe you get a great deal on tux rental. Just remember to keep your spending below the total amount you decide. You can apply this same strategy to planning for a class trip or saving for a concert.

> *Once you master managing a budget, you will have the tools to get on the right path for a successful financial future.*

Shortcuts

- ✓ Determine how much money you have coming in. Consider all of your income: paycheck, business income, monetary gifts, etc.

- ✓ List your expenses – rent/mortgage, food, gas, etc. Ask yourself: Which of these are needs?

- ✓ Give yourself a reasonable allowance so you can enjoy some of your wants.

- ✓ Create a money cushion. Ideally, you want to make sure you have some cash left after paying for essentials to put in a savings account reserved for emergencies.

- ✓ Adjust your spending. If you find that you are spending more than you make, you can either cut your expenses or try to bring in more income.

Sample Budget

	Budget Amount	Actual Amount	Budget - Actual
INCOME			
Paycheck			
Business Income			
Total Income			
EXPENSES			
Car payment			
Rent			
Car Insurance			
Groceries			
Cell Phone			
Utilities			
Entertainment			
Credit card			
Donations - Church			
Savings			
Total Expenses			
Income minus expenses			

CHAPTER 2

> ≫ Comparing Banks and Credit Unions

Having your own money creates a sense of independence, because you decide how much to spend or save.

Choosing the right financial institution is an important decision. Opening an account is painless. You provide your name, address, date of birth, some type of identifying document such as a driver's license, and your initial deposit. Then, you're ready to go. But how do you decide whether to stash your cash in a bank or credit union? Let's go over the benefits and drawbacks of each.

Banks versus Credit Unions

Banks are for-profit institutions, meaning they charge more for products to increase their earnings. They can have a national footprint like Bank of America or be more regional or community-focused. Credit unions, on the other hand, are non-profit organizations that tend to focus more on a particular region. Credit unions pay dividends (earnings paid out from its profits) to its members. The profits are also used to lower rates that members obtain on loans and increase returns they receive for deposits.

Almost anyone is eligible to open an account at a bank. Credit unions require a common bond for membership, such as being employed by a certain company or belonging to a particular organization. Additionally, all credit union account holders share ownership in the credit union and select the board of directors. Having an account at a bank does not make you a shareholder unless you decide to buy stock in that particular company.

One downside of credit unions is the limited availability of Automated Teller Machines (ATM). Most credit unions have a regional focus so if you are traveling out of that area, it may be difficult to find an ATM for your credit union. ATM cards are accepted at almost any machine, but most financial institutions charge a fee for customers who use their machines but don't have an account.

That's where banks have an edge. If you have an account at a national bank such as Citibank, Bank of America or Wachovia, there is a greater likelihood you will find an ATM if you are traveling across the country. Many banks and credit unions issue Visa/MasterCard Check cards which allow users to make purchases and have the costs deducted from checking account balances. In addition, using ATM cards for debit transactions allows consumers to withdraw cash at most retail stores without paying a fee. Just make sure no one is looking over your shoulder when you enter your personal identification number (PIN) (See Chapter 6 for more about identity theft). Whether you choose a bank or credit union, your deposits will be insured up to $100,000, meaning any balance under that level is protected even if the financial institution goes out of business.

Checking

Checking accounts are places to store cash used to pay for expenses. You can access the money two ways: by writing a check or by using an ATM/debit card. There are two basic types of checking accounts: interest-bearing and non-interest bearing. In exchange for paying you interest on your money, interest-bearing accounts require a minimum balance. If your balance falls beneath that level, the financial institution will likely charge a monthly fee until your account returns to your bank's balance requirement. Keep in mind that the interest rate paid on interest-bearing checking accounts is usually not that compelling. It varies depending on market conditions, but at the printing of this book the national average was 1.2% according to Bankrate.com. Non-interest bearing accounts typically require low or no minimum balance.

Money Market

A money market account is a type of checking account. These accounts typically pay a higher interest rate than checking or savings accounts (the national average was 2.9% at the printing of this book). Money market accounts make investments in short term funds. The return on the money is passed along to the account holders. This type of account, like interest-bearing checking accounts, usually requires a minimum balance, which can be anywhere from as low as $1 to as high as $50,000.

Savings

Savings accounts encourage customers to keep money in their accounts. They offer a higher interest rate than checking accounts.

Withdrawals and deposits are allowed, but no checks can be written against the balance.

Brokerage

This type of account is set up at an investment bank such as Merrill Lynch, Charles Schwab or Ameritrade. With a brokerage account you can buy and sell stocks, bonds, mutual funds and other investment vehicles. Most brokerage firms also permit customers to write checks against their account balance. (Brokerage accounts will be discussed more in chapter 12.)

Online Banking

Hate long lines? Feeling overwhelmed by stacks of paper like canceled checks and monthly statements? Online banking may be for you. It's the option of choice for a growing number of people. You could have your paycheck deposited directly into your checking account and never need to step into a bank. You can view your bank records online.

Some people worry about online banking because they think it makes their private information vulnerable to hackers. Banks are working to increase online banking security by using encryption software to protect sensitive information from being viewed by others. You can help safeguard your personal information by remembering to click the exit or logoff button at the end of an online session and close your Internet browser.

Some other features you can use through online banking:
- Check account balances.
- View current and historical transactions.
- See the front and back of checks that have been processed.
- Verify withdrawals and deposits.
- Stop payments on checks.
- Look at bank statements.
- Transfer funds between accounts.
- Download transactions to popular personal finance programs like Quicken and Microsoft Money.

All of these conveniences cut down on the amount of paper you receive in the mail. One less letter to file or shred helps a lot.

Online Bill Pay

A special feature of online banking that provides convenience and control is online bill pay. This option allows users the ability to receive and pay bills online. Some banks charge for this service, but many are starting to offer it for free. If you are working full time and living on your own, online bill pay is worth it even if you have to pay a small monthly fee.

Online bill pay allows you to view your bills and schedule payments. You can print a bill or bank statement if you want a hard copy. In the meantime, you save on postage by not having to buy stamps and frustration because you have less clutter.

Some online services will even send reminder e-mails to inform you that a bill is due. This is a great feature. When living on your own for the first time, it's nice to have something remind you that a bill is due. That nudge can mean the difference between having your lights on or getting them turned off. Restoring a canceled service means late fees and additional charges.

You can also set up recurring payments for your bills. For ones that are typically the same each month like rent/mortgage, cable, or car insurance, setting up a regular payment schedule can save time. Just specify the day of the month you want the money to be there and the funds will be sent automatically until you make a change.

Virtual Banks

Virtual banks are popping up everywhere. If you have no need to walk into a branch bank, this option can provide some nice benefits. Everything is handled online. Because these financial institutions don't have to employ tellers and other staff to operate several branches, they can pass the savings on to customers in the form of higher interest rates on checking and savings accounts. Virtual banks offer ATM cards, but because most don't own ATMs there is likely to be a fee every time you make a withdrawal. Another downside to these banks is that deposits can't be made via ATMs, so you may have to resort to using the mail, which can pose some security risks.

Bank Charges

Many banks offer free checking, but that does not mean everything is free. Here are some of the fees you may incur having a bank account:

Insufficient Funds — One day, you may accidentally write a check for more money than you have in your account. When someone tries to cash it, your bank will send you a notice of insufficient funds. That means your check has bounced. Everyone makes mistakes, but be careful not to willfully write bad checks because along with bank charges — which can be more than $30 per check — you could go to jail. The best way to keep from racking up bounced checks is to know what's coming in and out of your account. If your bank offers online banking, you can login to your account to verify which checks have cleared. You can also give yourself a safety net by finding out if your bank will allow your savings account to serve as overdraft protection. With that feature, if your checking account is short on money, the bank will draw cash from your savings account to cover the check. Another safeguard against bounced checks is considering the time it takes for your bank to make your money available after a deposit. Some banks may not allow you to access your funds for three to five days. If a check comes in during that time frame, it may bounce.

Wire Transfer – Say you're purchasing a house and need money transferred from your bank account to your lawyer's bank account, you may need to do a wire transfer. Fees for wire transfers can be as low as $10.

Stop Payment – If you write a check and realize you don't have enough money to cover the amount, you can stop payment on it. Charges often range from $15 to $30 for this service. Sounds high, but by stopping payment you can save the extra fees – and headaches — from charges for having insufficient funds.

ATM Fees – Think carefully about the ATM you use because you could pay a steep price if you choose one that's not owned by your bank. Some charge convenience fees as much as $5 per session.

Minimum Balance fees – As mentioned earlier, some banks charge fees if your checking or savings account balance dips below a certain level. The cost can be high, $20 or more per month in some cases.

Check fees – Some banks allow you to write a certain number of checks each month without a fee. If you exceed that limit, you will be charged a nominal amount of say 25 cents for each check. Remember to shop around for the best checking account for you. Plenty of banks offer unlimited check writing without a cost.

Final considerations

One last note on banking is: Do your homework and search for the financial institution that will best meet your needs. If you feel comfortable with the Internet and don't need to see a teller, virtual banks could be a good option. If you are planning to use a financial institution for loans and credit, credit unions might be the best option since they offer among the lowest rates on credit cards and loans. Their wide array of products and services can also be a selling point. Other factors in your decision could be availability of direct deposit, online banking and bill pay.

Also, think about fees. Banks and credit unions may require you to maintain a certain balance or pay a fee if you fall short. I recommend finding a firm that does not charge those kinds of penalties. Having to maintain a particular balance can be restrictive and costly. Some other fees to consider are wire transfer, stop payment and overdraft. My experience has been that credit unions are typically cheaper than banks in these fee categories by a wide margin.

Finally, consider convenience. If you will be using ATMs a lot or need to handle transactions in a physical location, choosing a bank with a big presence may be a good decision. Larger banks tend to have more ATMs than smaller banks, which can prevent you from having to pay ATM fees. Credit unions are usually local in nature so if you do a lot of ATM withdrawals, you may have to do a lot of searching to find one that doesn't charge a fee.

Just for Teens

If you've been waiting to open a checking account or even if you've never considered it, now is a good time to get going. As you progress through high school, money becomes more important. It makes sense to set up a checking account and store cash there on a regular basis. If you're like me, the more money you have in your wallet, the more you spend.

1 Whether you receive an allowance or have a job, allocate a portion of your money to go to your checking account. If your bank has online banking, sign up for that service. As mentioned earlier, you can view all deposits and withdrawals for your account. This helps immensely in balancing your checkbook.

2 Balancing your checkbook means you match your actual transactions (recorded in your check book) to what appears on your bank statement. Banks and vendors do make mistakes, so it is good to check your transactions on a regular basis. I have had situations where I used my debit card and was charged twice for the same purchase. So it is good to check your records at least weekly with online banking to verify everything is correct. Balancing a checkbook can take a long time if you have to wait until you receive your statement in the mail, but being able to view transactions every day with online banking can make the process easier and more efficient.

> *Balancing a checkbook can take a long time if you have to wait until you receive your statement in the mail, but being able to view transactions every day with online banking can make the process easier and more efficient.*

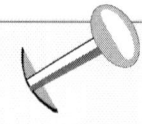

Shortcuts

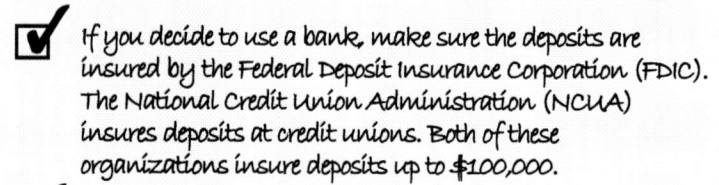

- ☑ If you decide to use a bank, make sure the deposits are insured by the Federal Deposit Insurance Corporation (FDIC). The National Credit Union Administration (NCUA) insures deposits at credit unions. Both of these organizations insure deposits up to $100,000.

- ☑ Find banks with flexible or extended branch hours. Not everyone works from 9 a.m. to 5 p.m. It's nice to have an account at a financial institution that has evening hours or is open on weekends.

- ☑ See if the bank offers credit cards. Compare the interest rates with other credit card companies to learn whether the rates are competitive.

- ☑ Ask whether the financial institution offers debit cards that bear either the Visa or MasterCard logo. Find out how the card is protected in the event it is lost or stolen.

- ☑ Learn what types of accounts are offered. You may want to consider a bank that has a wide range of accounts. That way, if your needs change, you have options to meet your requirements.

- ☑ Find out if the account you open requires a minimum balance. If so, make sure you maintain that amount. If you fall short, you will be charged fees. Some banks waive the minimum balance if you set up a direct deposit of your wages or other income into the account on a regular basis.

- ☑ Avoid banks that charge fees for withdrawing. Why should you pay to get your own money?

PART 2

> On-the-Road Experience

CHAPTER 3

≫ Understanding Credit

Without a credit card, it's tough to get even an airline ticket or hotel reservation. If you want to shop online, a credit card is almost a necessity.

Some people get their first taste of credit through offers received at college. Others get advertisements in the mail after working a first job. It feels powerful to go into a store and lay down a piece of plastic to pay for purchases. But too few of us consider that the financial choices we make today will affect opportunities to buy things we need in the future.

Three out of four college students have at least one credit card, according to Nellie Mae, a corporation that provides loans for education. On average, each student owes more than $2,000. By graduation, more than half of students have four or more credit cards, Nellie Mae found.

Credit is a good thing if managed properly. But so many people, myself included, abuse it at some point in their lives. We make charges without considering the consequences of buying more than we can afford. Out-of-control credit habits can lead to high interest rates and even losing the right to use that card. Think about how much tougher it would to be book an airline ticket, rent a car or make a hotel reservation without a credit card. And you can almost forget about shopping online.

Get a strong start by choosing the right card for you. Protect yourself by looking for those with low interest rates. Interest is what credit card companies charge on balances left unpaid after the grace period (the number of days you have to pay your bill in full before accruing extra charges). The grace period typically ranges from 1 to 30 days.

Next, search for cards with "zero" or low annual fees. An exception to this are reward cards, where you can earn airline miles, points or cash back based on your purchases. If this is important to you, be sure that you will charge enough to make your reward worth more than the fee (sometimes as high as $100 per year).

It helps to think of credit cards as loans. The issuer allows you to borrow money to make your purchases. That company wants something in return. That's where interest comes in. Many companies will drastically increase your interest rate if you pay your bill late. I know of cases where a 10% interest rate jumped to 26% because of one late payment. Paying your credit card bills in full and on time not only boosts your credit score, but it's like getting a loan interest-free.

Types of Credit

According to Wikipedia, an online encyclopedia, the financial definition of credit means "the granting of a loan or creation of debt." Loans and other outstanding amounts are meant to be repaid. The lender expects to receive the principal amount back, plus interest. For example, if you were to borrow $100 at 10% interest, the bank would expect to get $110 at the end of 12 months. The $100 is the principal amount; the amount that was borrowed. The $10 is the interest, or the bank's charge for letting you borrow the money. A loan is made for a specific time period and the interest payment is spread equally over the loan. This scenario is an example of simple interest.

Credit cards are a form of revolving credit, which means there are no fixed payments or loan periods. If you have no balance, you owe nothing. But if you have a lot of charges, you could pay for several years before eliminating your debt.

Credit card companies use compounding interest. That means unless you pay your balance in full, interest charges are added each month to what you owe, and interest is calculated on that new balance. In other words, you are paying interest on interest.

Let's say you have a card with 30% interest, and this interest is compounded daily. This means that for each day it carries a balance, you will be charged 0.08% per day. Sounds like no big deal, right? But as new charges are added, the credit card company will compound more interest on top of that. Before long, you could end up with a huge bill. Consider a $1,000 credit card balance with a 30% interest rate. If you make just a minimum payment of $30 per month, it will take 6 years to pay off your debt.

One way to keep interest from building is to avoid the trap of the monthly minimum. Paying that amount — just 2% to 4% of your total balance — can make you feel like you owe less than you really do.

Remember, credit cards shouldn't be used to extend your income. If you keep coming up short on money to pay for your charges, stop using that card until you get your finances under control. If you use credit cards for luxuries, such as vacations or holiday gifts, be sure to have a plan for paying off the balance quickly.

When you pay more than the monthly minimum, you are paying down the principal balance of the loan and freeing yourself from the cycle of debt. The lower the principal balance, the less interest the credit card company charges. Here's another way to look at it: The quicker you pay off your balance, the more you save, the more you win.

When you receive a credit card in the mail, you'll receive a document that spells out the terms, as well. That's the disclosure statement. Hold on to it. It goes over the benefits and penalties of your credit card. Remember to read the fine print. There you'll find information about how much your interest rate may increase if you pay your bill late. The tables on the following pages highlight the difference an interest rate increase can make on a $1,000 balance:

So remember to pay credit card bills on time, and pay more than the monthly minimum. If you pay just the minimum, additional charges can make the problem seem unbeatable.

Credit card A has a 15% interest rate and a monthly minimum payment of $25. If you accrue no additional charges and pay the minimum of $25 a month, you will pay off the $1,000 owed in 56 months (over 4 ½ years). The balance will be gone, but consider the cost: you'll have paid an extra $395 in interest! Conversely, if you double your payment to $50 per month, you will pay it off over two years (24 months) and pay $158 in interest.

Credit card A charges 15% interest and has monthly minimum payment of $25

Day	Balance	Payment	Daily Interest	Cumulative Interest
1	$1,000.00			
2	$1,000.41		$0.4110	$0.41
3	$1,000.82		$0.4111	$0.82
4	$1,001.23		$0.4113	$1.23
5	$1,001.64		$0.4115	$1.64
6	$1,002.06		$0.4116	$2.06
7	$1,002.47		$0.4118	$2.47
8	$1,002.88		$0.4120	$2.88
9	$1,003.29		$0.4121	$3.29
10	$1,003.70		$0.4123	$3.70
11	$1,004.12		$0.4125	$4.12
12	$1,004.53		$0.4127	$4.53
13	$1,004.94		$0.4128	$4.94
14	$1,005.36		$0.4130	$5.36
15	$1,005.77		$0.4132	$5.77
16	$1,006.18		$0.4133	$6.18
17	$1,006.60		$0.4135	$6.60
18	$1,007.01		$0.4137	$7.01
19	$1,007.42		$0.4138	$7.42
20	$1,007.84		$0.4140	$7.84
21	$1,008.25		$0.4142	$8.25
22	$1,008.67		$0.4143	$8.67
23	$1,009.08		$0.4145	$9.08
24	$1,009.49		$0.4147	$9.49
25	$1,009.91		$0.4149	$9.91
26	$1,010.32		$0.4150	$10.32
27	$1,010.74		$0.4152	$10.74
28	$1,011.16		$0.4154	$11.16
29	$1,011.57		$0.4155	$11.57
30	$986.99	$25.00	$0.4157	$11.99

> Now, let's look at **credit card B.** Say you received a 26% interest rate because you were late with a payment. Interest builds each day. At the end of the month, you've racked up almost $21 in interest charges. Just making the monthly minimum payment of $25 will take more 7 ½ years to pay off the balance and cost you $1,350 in interest. However, if you double your payment to $50 per month, the whole situation changes. You would pay off your credit card in just over two years and save more than $1,000 in interest costs.

Types of Credit Cards

There are two main types of credit cards: unsecured and secured.

Unsecured Cards

Unsecured cards are the most popular credit cards. They don't require you to have any collateral. Credit is issued based upon your credit worthiness. Lenders will look at factors such as your credit score and income in determining how much credit to grant. If you decide to get an unsecured card, start with a low credit limit like $500. Again, try to pay off charges in full each month to avoid interest charges.

If you're unable to pay off the balance each month, make a plan to clear it within a certain time frame. Say you charge a $300 MP3 player and can only afford about $60 a month. That means you'd be able to pay it off in about five months. Remember: you'll be paying interest, so you'll end up paying back more than $300.

Credit card B charges 26% interest and has monthly minimum payment of $25

Day	Balance	Payment	Daily Interest	Cumulative Interest
1	$1,000.00			
2	$1,000.71		$ 0.7123	$0.71
3	$1,001.43		$ 0.7128	$1.43
4	$1,002.14		$ 0.7133	$2.14
5	$1,002.85		$ 0.7139	$2.85
6	$1,003.57		$ 0.7144	$3.57
7	$1,004.28		$ 0.7149	$4.28
8	$1,005.00		$ 0.7154	$5.00
9	$1,005.71		$ 0.7159	$5.71
10	$1,006.43		$ 0.7164	$6.43
11	$1,007.15		$ 0.7169	$7.15
12	$1,007.86		$ 0.7174	$7.86
13	$1,008.58		$ 0.7179	$8.58
14	$1,009.30		$ 0.7184	$9.30
15	$1,010.02		$ 0.7190	$10.02
16	$1,010.74		$ 0.7195	$10.74
17	$1,011.46		$ 0.7200	$11.46
18	$1,012.18		$ 0.7205	$12.18
19	$1,012.90		$ 0.7210	$12.90
20	$1,013.62		$ 0.7215	$13.62
21	$1,014.34		$ 0.7220	$14.34
22	$1,015.07		$ 0.7225	$15.07
23	$1,015.79		$ 0.7231	$15.79
24	$1,016.51		$ 0.7236	$16.51
25	$1,017.24		$ 0.7241	$17.24
26	$1,017.96		$ 0.7246	$17.96
27	$1,018.69		$ 0.7251	$18.69
28	$1,019.41		$ 0.7256	$19.41
29	$1,020.14		$ 0.7262	$20.14
30	$995.86	$25.00	$ 0.7267	$20.86

(* These examples assume no additional purchases were made.)

Secured Cards

Secured cards typically require you to back up your credit limit with a savings account. For example, a $500 limit would require maintaining a balance of $500 in your savings account. You would have to deposit more money into your savings account to increase your available credit. For those wishing to get their first credit card, a secured card is a wise choice. If the bill isn't paid, the bank will withdraw money from your savings account to pay the balance. This will help you learn to charge only what you can reasonably expect to pay back, thereby avoiding financial disaster. Secured credit cards also serve as a good stepping-stone to obtaining unsecured cards.

Debit Cards (also known as "check cards")

Although debit cards are not credit cards, they carry the Visa or MasterCard logo and allow you to make purchases, from which the cost is automatically deducted from your checking account. For many, check cards are more convenient than carrying a checkbook and are simply easier to use. When making purchases, you don't have to worry about wasting time looking for a pen or filling out your check.

If the transaction is done as a debit, all you have to do is enter your personal identification number (PIN). Debit cards can be used for Internet purchases, as well.

Also, because Visa and MasterCard are accepted worldwide, debit cards bearing those logos are usually accepted globally. They are a good option when you are learning to manage credit because no debt is involved. Additionally, they are not as restrictive as secured cards, which require maintaining a savings account with withdrawal limitations. One drawback to consider is that debit cards will not help you establish a credit history because how you use them is not reported to credit reporting agencies.

Other Types of Credit

Credit cards represent just one area you'll need to navigate on your path to financial freedom. Here are some others:

INSTALLMENT CREDIT

Mortgages and car loans are examples of installment credit. These types of loans require you to make fixed payments over a specific time period.

Similar to a secured credit card, which uses your savings account as a backup, your home or vehicle is pledged as collateral. If you fail to pay, the lender can take away your property through foreclosure. Your credit score will also plummet, making it harder to obtain credit in the future.

SERVICE BILLS

When you think about credit, you may not consider utility and cell phone bills. But that's what they are: agreements that you will pay for a specified service to receive some type of benefit. For example, if you have a gym membership, you have to pay the monthly bill to have the right to use the facilities. In many cases, failing to pay service bills on time will result in late payments being noted and tacked on to your credit report.

Line of Credit

A line of credit is similar to a credit card because you will only receive a bill if you use it. There are two main lines of credit for consumers: home equity and signature.

Home equity lines are secured by your residence. The credit available to you is determined by the amount of equity in your home. If, for example, your home is worth

$150,000 and your mortgage balance is $100,000, the equity is $50,000 ($150,000 - $100,000). If the balance of your line of credit is not paid, the lender can foreclose on the property.

A signature line of credit is unsecured and carries a higher interest rate than home equity lines. Lenders grant signature lines based on your credit history. People use them for a variety of reasons, such as for home improvements and paying off other bills. Also, if you have unexpected expenses and no cash, lines of credit can be helpful because they usually carry lower interest rates than cash advances from your credit card, and most other types of loans.

A word of caution: I would not suggest using a home equity line to consolidate bills such as car payments and credit card purchases. The interest rates and monthly payments are lower than some other credit and loan options, but you put your home at risk if you can't pay the bill.

Just as when shopping for credit cards, take the time to consider the benefits and risks of using a line of credit. If you decide the pluses outweigh the minuses, then look for the best terms. Just be sure to stop all optional spending until your debt is paid.

STUDENT LOANS

When I graduated from college, I had no job but owed $8,000 from student loans. I felt overwhelmed because I didn't know how I was going to pay that debt along with all of my other bills. Fortunately, I had a six-month grace period before payments were due. Before that term ended, I called my lender and explained my situation. My loan was placed in forbearance for three months. The good news: I didn't have to make any payments during that 90-day period.

The bad news: Interest accrued, so the total cost of my loan went up.

It helps to know what types of student loans are available and what the terms are. There are basically two types of student loans:

Subsidized – These are need-based loans. The government pays the interest while you are in school (provided you are enrolled at least on a half-time basis).

Unsubsidized – These are non-need based loans. You become solely responsible for the interest on the loan as soon as you receive the check.

Repayment Options

Equal Payment – This means you pay the principal and interest on your loans. The payments are fixed for the life of the loan.

Graduated Payment –These payments start low but increase at regular intervals, such as every two years. In the early years of the loan you're paying mostly interest, but over time, as your payment goes up, a bigger portion will go toward paying the principal.

Income-sensitive – In this case, your payment is based on a percentage of your income. The amount can range from as low as 4% of your salary to as much as 25%. As with graduated loans, this option offers lower payment amounts to ease your transition to the workforce, but it increases the overall costs because more interest accumulates before the loan is paid in full.

Consolidation

Consolidation is another way to lower your monthly student loan payments. If you have several loans or want to lock in a certain interest rate, consolidating your loans can create a more manageable bill.

Here's how it works: The lender will issue a check to pay for all of your student loans. It then creates a new loan for you with a new repayment schedule. These loans can be spread over 25 years.

Loan Tips

Before skipping a payment on your student loan, talk with your lender to determine if it will offer a repayment plan that fits your budget. This is very important, because failing to pay your bill on time will be noted on your credit report. Some lenders will offer a reduction in your interest rate or cash and rewards for paying your bill on time over a specified time period (usually at least 24 consecutive months).

I know how tough it is to pay bills right out of college, but it's important to develop your own repayment plan that pays more than your lender requires. Ideally, you want to pay more than the monthly minimum payment to cut down on your repayment period and lower your interest costs.

Think about it this way: If you have a student loan with a $25,000 balance, a 6% annual interest rate and a minimum payment of $245, it would take 12 years to pay off your debt. However, if you increase your payment to $300 per month, it will knock three years off your schedule and free up your money for other things.

Types of Credit to Avoid

Next, we will explore payday, auto title, and refund anticipation loans. Put simply, here's the best advice: Don't use them. But if you have no other option, consider them as short-term loans that you need to repay within one month. Because the fees are high, you should not consider these loans if you can't pay them off within 30 days.

Payday Loans

You've probably seen the advertisements either on TV or in spam e-mail for loans to help you make it until payday. These are short-term loans with very high interest rates. These companies prey on people who are struggling financially or have credit problems. As long as you have a steady paycheck and a checking account, you can get a payday loan.

Here's how it works: You give your contact information. You tell the company how much you want to borrow. (These companies typically lend up to $500.) Next, you write a post-dated check or authorize the payday lender to debit your account. Finally, you receive your much-needed cash, minus the fees (which range from $15-$30 per $100 borrowed). Sounds simple enough.

Let's break it down. Consider a fee of $15 per $100 borrowed. That translates into an annual percentage rate of almost 400%. Say you borrow $300 and your fee is $45. That means you're really getting just $255 in your pocket. When payday arrives, your check is cashed to satisfy the loan. If you're like many borrowers who can't really afford to pay the loan, you'll have to get a new one from the lender and start the cycle again.

If you continue this pattern for eight pay periods, you will have paid $615 ($255 + $315 in fees {45 * 8}). That's means you've paid for your $300 loan twice!

If you lack the cash in your account to cover the post-dated check the lender is holding, you risk having your check bounce. This will cause even more fees. The bank and the payday lender can charge you for having insufficient funds and threaten legal action.

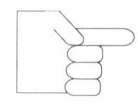

Consider these facts carefully, cited from the Center for Responsible Lending:

- *Five million payday borrowers fall into this debt trap each year.*
- *Ninety-one percent of all payday loans are made to borrowers with five or more payday loans.*
- *The average payday borrower is refinanced eight times by a single lender paying $800 to borrow $325.*

AUTO TITLE LOANS

Auto title loans are short-term loans, typically 30 days or fewer. If you own your vehicle, you could use it to obtain this type of loan. Auto title loan companies don't bother to check your credit because they require you to provide a set of keys, which they will use to repossess your vehicle if you default on the loan. Loan amounts are determined by the fair market value of your car, but are far less than its worth. You can go to the Kelley Blue Book Web site (www.kbb.com) to get an estimate of your vehicle's worth.

Loan amounts are usually at least $600, but no more than $2,500. The interest rate on the loan could be 30%, but that rate is for one month. So, if you have a $500 loan, the interest would be $150 ($500 * 30%). You would therefore owe $650 at the end of the month.

If you can't pay the full amount, the lender will roll the loan over to the next month. So, if you are only able to pay the $150 in interest, the next month you will owe $650 on top of the money you already paid because the interest is continuing to increase at a rate of 30% each month.

Refund Anticipation Loans

Have you ever seen TV ads or heard radio announcements from companies promising to deliver your tax refund the same day? These companies are really offering loans. They give you an advance against your refund, but it comes at a cost - a steep one. Fees for processing the loan and preparing your tax forms can easily top $200 in some cases. It may seem like a small price to pay if you have a big refund and want to get your funds fast, but that money that could have helped pay down a credit card bill or student loan.

Instead of rushing for the quick payout, consider using online tax preparation companies which are part of the IRS's Free File program. They will file your tax return electronically for free if you meet certain requirements. Check http://www.irs.gov for more details. Often, you can get your refund between eight to 15 days. If you don't have access to the Internet you can also receive free tax preparation at your local IRS office if your annual income is less than $38,000. Most locations also offer free electronic filing. Call your local IRS office for details. The bottom line is to avoid these expensive loans and be patient to so you can receive all of your refund.

Payday, auto title, and refund anticipation loans underscore the need for developing a budget and building up an emergency fund to "cushion" you in the event you are short on cash. If you don't have any cash left after paying your bills, you need to adjust your spending habits so you can build up enough savings to avoid falling into these traps.

Here are some tips from the Consumer Federation of America on handling cash crunches without borrowing

- Before you are late on a rent, mortgage, or utility payment, speak with the creditor. For non-interest bills, such as utility or telephone bills, ask about making payment arrangements. Ask to delay payment until your paycheck arrives or set up a repayment schedule that stretches out payments. Make sure to ask about fees or extra costs for extended payments.

- Delay expensive items until you have cash. If a car repair is causing the cash-flow problem, explore public transportation options until you have the funds together to repair your vehicle. See if any co-workers live nearby so that you can car-pool to work.

- Apply for assistance programs, such as emergency utility funds. Take advantage of local charity, religious, or community programs that help families make ends meet in a crisis.

- Work overtime or pick up extra work to bring in more income. Sell something of value that you no longer need.

- Consider adjusting the amount withheld for taxes to provide more money in your paycheck instead of over-withholding every payday to get a big tax refund later.

Just for Teens

1 To get a feel for how credit works, try starting out with a secured credit card. First, you will have to open a savings account and make a deposit. The balance in the account is your credit limit.

2 Begin with a low limit like $300. If you are under 18, you will have to get a parent or guardian to co-sign. That means they will be responsible for the bill if you don't pay. For teens in this situation, remember that not paying your bill on time will not only hurt your credit history, but also your parents'.

3 Once you have your credit card, use it to make at least one small purchase monthly, and pay it off in full. Regular charges such as $15 for gas or $10 for snacks can go a long way toward establishing a good credit history – that is, if you pay the bill on time.

4 To help you stay current, sign up to receive an electronic bill from the credit card company. The company will send you an e-mail to remind you the bill is due.

> *When you are busy, it is easy to let some things fall through the cracks. Don't let your credit card bill be one of them.*

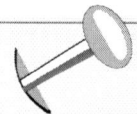

Shortcuts

☑ If you use a credit card, remember that the amount you owe is a loan and must be repaid. If you don't pay the bill on time, you can damage your credit history, thus making it tougher to get credit in the future.

☑ If you are just starting out, try an unsecured credit card with a low limit ($500 or less). This gives you a chance to try things out to determine whether you are ready to handle a higher limit in the future.

☑ Secured cards require a savings account, which serves as your credit limit and becomes collateral if you fail to pay your bill on time.

☑ Shop around for the card that best meets your needs.

☑ Avoid payday, auto title, and refund anticipation loans. If you need cash and don't have an emergency fund, consider using a line of credit to help your short-term needs. Then create a plan to pay it off as soon as possible.

CHAPTER 4

> ≫ Breaking Down Credit Reports

Each month, your payment history is shared with major reporting companies such as Experian, Equifax and TransUnion. Do you pay on time?

What's the lowdown on credit reports? Why do they matter? If you've ever had a credit card application declined, you already know. They can create – or crush – a chance to obtain credit.

Are you repeatedly late? All of this information gets logged on your report. And here's another reason to care: The positives — and the missteps — stay on your report for years.

Here are the major sections of a credit report:

Personal Information

This segment details identifying information such as your name, address and Social Security number. It also lists your current and past employers.

Account Information

This is the part where, if you've managed credit well, looking at your record should make you proud. If you've stumbled, get ready for a jolt. Everything is here — the accounts you pay on time, the bills you blow off, the accounts you closed or forgot you had. You'll find information on your car loans, mortgages, credit cards, student and other types of loans. Each account shows the amount of your credit line, payment history and how much you owe.

Public Records

If you have been involved in legal action over a debt, such as a judgment or bankruptcy, or if you have had a tax lien filed against you, it will be reported in this section. These items are collected routinely from court records.

Inquiries

Inquiries are records of who has had access to your credit report. There are two types. The first occurs when you apply for credit or a financial service in which your report is reviewed to help make the decision. The

---

How long will information remain on your credit report?

Open account in good standing	Indefinitely
Late or missed payment	7 years
Collection accounts	7 years
Chapter 7 bankruptcy	10 years
Chapter 13 bankruptcy	7 years
Unpaid tax liens	15 years
Paid tax lien	7 years
Credit inquiries	2 years

Source: Experian

other is shown only to you. This would happen, for instance, when you obtain a copy of your own report.

As you can see in the table on the previous page, late payments remain on your credit report for seven years. The "clock" for collection accounts starts from the date of the first missed payment that led to the account being turned over to a collection agency. Typically, after about 120 days, a bill will be sent to collections.

For example, if you missed your credit card payment in January 2006, the account would have gone into collection in April. In this case, both the original and collection accounts would be deleted in January 2013.

CREDIT SCORES

Contrary to popular belief, a credit report does not rate your credit. It provides a history of your accounts, how much you owe and how you have paid over time. To make that information meaningful, companies have turned to credit scoring. A credit scoring model is formed by analyzing many credit histories that are similar to yours. These scores give creditors a tool to determine what your payment patterns will likely be and how to set your terms.

There are thousands of different scoring models. Some are designed to predict general risk. Others are risk-specific, such as for car loans, insurance, retail credit, etc. Often a score is known by the name of the company that developed it.

For example, one well-known developer of scores is the Fair Isaac Corporation (FICO). FICO models are often used in the mortgage industry. They have adopted a fairly set approval/denial numbering scale. However, this has led consumers to mistakenly believe that there is only one scoring model with a defined approval scale for all lenders.

Here's how it really works: Each of the three credit reporting companies — Equifax, Experian, and TransUnion, as well as FICO, offer a scoring service to consumers. From any of their Web sites, you can purchase an educational score which will help you understand where your credit history falls in the range of risk.

A mark of 750 (generally considered very good) can easily fall to the lower 500s (regarded as poor) if credit bills are not paid on time, so try not to get hung up on monitoring your current score. As long as you understand the risk factors that influenced the score, you'll have the information you need to be credit-smart.

Because reports vary, there are no rules for how much one factor will affect your score. But here are some issues that will most influence your risk position or score:

1. Payment history. Missed payments will hurt your credit report more than any other factor. Within this category, it is even more negative if the missed payments were recent and if there were several missed payments instead of just one. The older they are in your history, the less significant they become. Collection accounts and public records, however, will have a major impact for as long as they remain in your report.

2. Utilization, or balance-to-limit ratio. Carrying high balances relative to your total credit limit is a sign of risk. Say you have a $4,000 balance on a credit card with a $5,000 limit and three other cards with an additional $15,000 in available credit. You are using only 20% of your existing credit limit ($4,000/$20,000). The scoring model would give you a higher score than someone who has only one card with a $4,000 balance on a $5,000 limit. Even though you have a high balance on one card, you have used a much smaller percentage of your total available credit. The person who has only $5,000 in available credit has used 80% of his or her existing credit ($4,000/$5,000). Because the scoring models work like this, keep cards in good standing open, even if you have no balance.

3. Types of accounts. Lenders like to see customers who can handle different types of credit (e.g., credit cards, car loans, mortgage loans). Your payment history on credit cards is the most important because, unlike automobile and mortgage loans, which have the same payment amount each month, credit card payments change based on your usage. If you can manage multiple types of accounts and pay bills on time, this shows that you know how to manage your credit, which will increase your score.

4. Inquiries. Recent inquiries (up to six months) indicate that you may have opened accounts which have not yet been reported in your account history. That potential debt is an unknown risk as far as the lender is concerned. If you are planning to buy a house or car soon, don't open several new accounts because it will lower your score.

You can get a free estimate of your FICO score at www.bankrate.com/brm/fico/calc.asp. This site will list a range into which your score may fall.

In addition to the Web sites noted above, another useful source of information is www.nationalscoreindex.com. This site is sponsored by Experian and will allow you to check the average Experian score by a particular state, region, or zip code.

It's important to remember that lenders use different credit scoring models when determining whether to grant credit. A credit score you access for a fee from the Internet may be totally different from the score a lender is looking at when you apply for a loan. Car insurance companies, for example, will look at a model that gives more weight to your past claims.

If you are applying for a car loan, the lender will focus more on your past automobile payment history.

In the past, lenders used a paper-and-pencil formula to determine whether to grant credit. If you had a short credit history, you might have been rejected because there wasn't enough data to assess. The benefit of credit risk scoring models is that they strike a balance between negative factors, such as a brief credit history, and positive factors, like paying your bills on time, to generate a score — regardless of the length of your credit history.

DISPUTES

Sometimes your creditors may not update your payments to credit reporting agencies on a timely manner. This can cause your credit history to be incorrect. Check your report at least annually. If you find an error, use online services, automated phone systems or write a letter to the credit reporting companies to challenge the information.

Once a dispute is requested, the company will contact the lender who reported the information and ask them to verify or update it. If the lender doesn't respond or confirm the information within 30 days, it will be removed from your credit report.

If your identifying information, such as your name, is spelled incorrectly, it may be updated immediately. In some cases, proof of your identity will be required to protect you from fraud. Be diligent with follow-up calls and other contacts to make sure your credit report reflects accurate information. Remember: it will follow you the rest of your life.

Some services claim to legally remove information from your credit report by sending several letters

The three major credit reporting agencies:

Equifax   (800) 685-1111   www.equifax.com
Experian   (888) 397-3742   www.experian.com
Trans Union (800) 888-4213   www.transunion.com

disputing an account in hopes that the creditor will fail to respond within 30 days and the account will be deleted. Don't waste your money. These scams are illegal!

Getting a Copy of Your Credit Report

Starting in 2005, credit reporting companies were required by Federal law to create a place for consumers to obtain one free credit report per year. Get yours by calling (877) 322-8228, or by visiting www.annualcreditreport.com.

In addition, many companies offer online credit reports, scores and monitoring services. They obtain the reports from one of the three national companies. These products can be used to monitor your credit report on a more frequent basis to help spot fraud.

All of these resources make it easy to examine your credit report and verify that your information is correct. Here's what can happen if you don't: My brother was named after my dad, and there was a situation in which some of his debts showed up on my father's credit report. This problem was corrected after the creditor noticed they had different Social Security numbers. Remember to check credit reports at least once a year.

Just for Teens

1 Still unclear about credit reports? It may help to compare it to a library record. A library will consider your borrowing history before allowing you to check out more books. A credit card company will check out your credit report before offering you more credit.

2 If you owe too much on your credit cards, you may be turned down when you apply for a new one, just as if you're at your limit of borrowed books, a library will stop you from taking home another one until the ones you have are returned. Both libraries and creditors have late fees. But the latter takes an extra step.

> If you are late with your payments, creditors note it on your credit report. This negative information will stay there for several years.

Shortcuts

(How to increase your credit score)

- ☑ Pay bills on time. One 30-day late payment can have a damaging effect on your credit report.

- ☑ Use credit sensibly. Try to keep balances lower than 50% of your available limit.

- ☑ Leave accounts in good standing open. These records stay on your credit report indefinitely and help improve your score.

- ☑ Limit credit inquiries. While it's OK to check your credit report periodically, don't apply for new credit too often within a short time frame.

CHAPTER 5

> **≫ Navigating Credit Problems**

If you are in a situation where you can't make your credit card payments, talk to the issuer of the card. Most are willing to work with you.

Many people have problems paying bills on time at some point in their lives. I've had my share of cash crunches. But I always found a way to bounce back and so can you. These companies would rather receive something than nothing. Making a payment arrangement can preserve your credit rating.

Each time you are late with credit payments, the issuer makes a note on your credit report. Notations are made for 30, 60, 90 and 120 days past due. Each mark hurts your credit score and makes it more difficult to obtain credit for purchases such as a car or house. In this chapter, we'll discuss some strategies for overcoming credit troubles.

Charge-offs

Typically, if a bill has been unpaid for four months, the company will charge it off to bad debt in their records and sell the account, at a reduced amount, to a collection agency. At this point the creditor no longer owns the account, but you still owe the bill. You can expect calls and/or letters from the collection agency demanding payment. If you'd like to negotiate a settlement, call and work out the details. It's best if the collection agency agrees to delete your debt once you pay the agreed-upon amount, because that means all of those late payment notations will be removed as well. Also, ask for a letter outlining the agreement before sending any money.

Both the original account and the collection account will be a part of your credit report, and both will be deleted at the same time — 7 years from the date of the first missed payment that led to the charge-off.

If you plan to rent an apartment or buy a house or car, having even one collection account can cause you to be rejected or receive a high interest rate because it "brands" you as a high-risk customer; i.e., someone who does not pay credit card bills on time.

Credit Counselors

Some people turn to credit counselors for help when debt becomes unbearable. These organizations will review your bills and assist you in consolidating them into one payment, often with a lower interest rate than your individual credit cards. Creditors often fund credit counseling programs because it protects their interests. Lenders would rather work with counselors, even if it means accepting lower payments, than be paid nothing.

Some people seek credit counseling as a way of avoiding bankruptcy. To find a reputable credit counselor close to you, check the National Foundation for Credit Counseling (www.nfcc.org). This organization sets standards for credit counseling companies and requires them to undergo accreditation every four years. In addition, it has a certification process for credit counselors to ensure they are providing education while upholding ethical standards.

Credit Repair Scams

"Eradicate card payments and see zero balances. Cancel debts and never make another payment!"

"Discharge debts quickly, painlessly, legally. For the rest of the story about canceling debt, go to our elimination page."

These are excerpts from just a few bogus e-mails I have received. If you receive similar letters or e-mails or hear ads on the radio or TV making such claims, remember the old saying: "If it sounds too good to be true, it probably is."

Always beware of firms that promise you the world. For a fee, some companies claim to erase bankruptcies and other bad credit. There is no legal way to remove accurate information on a credit report. If there is an error, you can request an investigation, but that's a free service.

According to the Credit Repair Organizations Act, credit repair firms cannot advise you to commit illegal acts like changing one letter in your name to create a new credit file or sending several letters disputing an account you know to be correct in hopes the creditor will fail to verify the debt within 30 days, thereby deleting the account from your report.

One last point on credit repair firms is that they cannot charge for a service they promise until they fully deliver. If the company says, for instance, that it will eliminate bad debts from your credit report, you do not have to pay until they have delivered on their claim.

Some firms will ask you to pay a monthly fee while they work on repairing your credit file. Below is an excerpt from the Federal Trade Commission:

"You have a right to dispute inaccurate information in your credit report by contacting the credit bureau directly. However, neither you nor any 'credit repair' company or credit repair organization has the right to have accurate, current, and verifiable information removed from your credit report. The credit bureau must remove accurate, negative information from your report only if it is over 7 years old. Bankruptcy information can be reported for 10 years."
   Source: Federal Trade Commission

This basically means you don't need a middle man. You can do anything a legitimate credit repair organization can. Since you spent the time charging up the debts, be the one to tackle the problem.

Consistently paying your bills on time is the best way to maintain and improve your score.

Bankruptcy

According to the American Heritage Dictionary, bankruptcy is a voluntary petition where you are judged to be legally insolvent. This basically means that you lack the money to pay your debts.

People file for protection under bankruptcy laws for a number of reasons. Some of the more common include credit card debt, job loss, medical bills, divorce or bad financial management.

Bankruptcy may be your choice or forced upon you by creditors. It can cause debts to either be eliminated or repaid under the direction of the bankruptcy court.

For individuals, there are two basic types of bankruptcy: Chapter 7 and Chapter 13. Those designations refer to their particular chapters within Title 11 of the United States Code.

Chapter 7 is often referred to as liquidation because it allows certain debts to be eliminated. In some cases, property may be sold to pay down debts. But some states prohibit the selling of certain assets such as cars and houses for Chapter 7 bankruptcy purposes. In states where cars are not exempt, they can be repossessed, but the consumer has the right to continue making the payments.

It's important to understand that bankruptcy doesn't wipe away all debts. Items such as child support, tax obligations and student loans are typically not forgiven.

Chapter 13 is referred to as reorganization. This type of bankruptcy allows filers the chance to repay debts by adjusting loan terms. If you have a debt such as a mortgage payment, Chapter 13 gives you the option of catching up on missed payments by spreading the debt out over a longer period of time. The length of repayment depends on the amount owed.

Changes in Bankruptcy Law

In October 2005, a new law was established to require individuals to receive a certificate from a credit counselor before filing for bankruptcy. The purpose of this is to make sure consumers have no other way to pay back the funds before taking such a drastic step as filing for bankruptcy, and to ensure they have learned how to budget and manage their expenses so they aren't repeat filers.

Credit counselors must be approved by the U.S. Trustee Program, which oversees the bankruptcy courts in the United States. Consumers receive counseling on budgeting before and after filing.

There are changes to Chapter 7 bankruptcy, too. It's no longer an automatic way to eliminate debts. First, the law exempts certain living expenses like food and rent/mortgage payments from a formula to determine whether a consumer can afford to pay a portion of unsecured debt like credit card bills.

Next, your income will be compared to the state median. If it exceeds that amount, you will not be allowed to file a liquidation bankruptcy. This is to ensure that consumers who can afford to repay a portion of their debts do so through a Chapter 13 bankruptcy rather than totally walking away from what they owe.

One last note on the changes is the increase in attorney's fees. The new laws require that more data be obtained, and lawyers are required to vouch that the information submitted to the courts is accurate. Therefore, lawyers' fees may become higher. If it is discovered that information the lawyer reported to the bankruptcy court is false, legal action can be taken against you and your lawyer.

The purpose of the new laws is to promote good financial management skills. There is another adage well worth repeating: "If you give a man a fish, you feed him for a day, but if you teach him how to fish, you feed him for a lifetime." Many people have not been taught how to properly manage their personal finances, and the government's hope is that good credit counseling will get folks back on the right track and help them avoid filing for bankruptcy again in the future.

Keep in mind, bankruptcies can remain on a credit report up to 10 years. This can make it difficult to obtain credit in the future. As I mentioned earlier, you can contact creditors directly if you are unable to make payments on time, and you can set up a repayment schedule without going to credit counselors or filing for bankruptcy.

Just for Teens

1 Credit card companies market aggressively to teens, so there is a good chance you may receive an offer for one before you finish high school. Nothing is wrong with having a credit card. It's how you use it that counts.

I got my first credit card when I was 18 and had another one before my 20th birthday. I ran my credit to the limit and didn't pay the bills on time. The accounts were turned over to collection agencies, which harassed me for payment.

2 Paying your bills late or irregularly can affect not only your ability to get new credit, but also your ability to get a job. Certain occupations that deal with money may check your credit report and reject you if you have a bad credit history.

3 Problems with credit can also affect your ability to get an apartment. After I graduated from college, I had a tough time getting a place of my own because of my checkered credit history. With negative marks on your credit report, you also may not be able to get car insurance, or you may be forced to pay a high premium.

> Just remember that the financial decisions you make today will affect you in the future, so use credit wisely.

Shortcuts

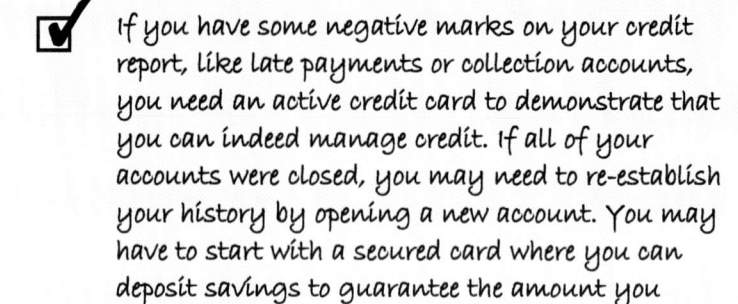

- [x] If you have some negative marks on your credit report, like late payments or collection accounts, you need an active credit card to demonstrate that you can indeed manage credit. If all of your accounts were closed, you may need to re-establish your history by opening a new account. You may have to start with a secured card where you can deposit savings to guarantee the amount you charge on the card. Make one or two small purchases each month and pay the bill off. Over time, this will improve your credit score.

- [x] Check your credit report periodically to make sure your information is accurate.

- [x] If your credit card bills are so high you can only pay the monthly minimum, re-read Chapter 1 of this book to learn more about budgeting or seek the help of a credit counseling company that offers money management advice or classes. Stop charging until you get your balance under control.

- [x] Filing for Chapter 7 bankruptcy (liquidation) has gotten tougher. The government is steering more people toward Chapter 13 (reorganization), which essentially sets up a payment plan to pay for debts, as opposed to Chapter 7, which completely erases and relieves you of the debt.

Dear Sir or Madam:

I recently received a copy of my credit report and discovered that it contains inaccurate information.

Account XYZ: Is not my account
Account ABC: I have never been late on this account

My full name is: John Smith
My Social Security number is: 123-45-6789
My date of birth is: April 1, 1987
My address is: 57 Swordfish Lane, Anywhere, FL. 32450

Please investigate this matter, correct and delete the inaccurate information from my credit file and send me an updated credit report.

If you have any questions feel free to give me a call at (XXX) 867-5309 or email me at **info@patrickalyons.com**

Thank you for your attention to this matter.

Sincerely,

John Smith

CHAPTER 6

≫ Avoiding Identity Theft

Identity thieves are very clever at finding ways to steal your personal information. But there are ways to reduce your risk of becoming a victim.

You go through last month's mail and try to clear some of the clutter. You throw away old bills without a thought. But you should think about what you're doing. Thieves rummage through trash looking for any bit of personal information. Some will pilfer your credit card number. Others will swipe your Social Security and bank account numbers. They will assume your identity, steal and commit fraud in your name.

Identity theft is becoming rampant in America. According to the Consumer Sentinel report published by Federal Trade Commission, the number of complaints was up more than 26% between 2002 and 2005. In 2005, there were more than 686,000 cases of identity theft and fraud cases reported, costing consumers more than $680 million.

How do you protect yourself? Identity theft occurs when someone has access to your identification information. The first move is making sure you cut up receipts and bills with details such as your name, address and account numbers with a cross shredder.

This makes it almost impossible for a thief to reassemble the document.

Another safeguard is checking your credit report for errors and signs of suspicious activity. The major credit bureaus, Equifax, Experian and TransUnion, all have monitoring services that allow users to receive updates on changes that may alert you to identity theft. According to a report published by the Identity Theft Resource Center, a growing amount of the pilfering is committed among family members. Surprisingly, the most common reported cases are parents using their child's information to obtain credit or services such as phone and utilities. Sadly, many young people are going to pay for these mistakes by having bad credit history before they're even old enough to apply for credit themselves.

Types of Fraud

FINANCIAL IDENTITY

If you have credit cards or bank accounts, you could potentially become a victim of financial identity fraud. This occurs when someone tries to either swindle money from your existing accounts or establish new ones in your name. Some criminals will steal your personal checks to purchase goods. These checks will bounce if you don't have enough funds in your account. Criminals can also use your credit or debit cards to steal from you. In 2001, someone used golfer Tiger Woods' identity – his name and Social Security number — to pilfer $17,000 worth of merchandise. In 2005, an impostor stole rapper/actor Will Smith's identity and charged nearly $33,000 worth of goods.

CRIMINAL IDENTITY

Criminal identity theft occurs when a person assumes your identity and violates the law. The imposter may have some type of ID bearing your name and decides to rob a bank, retail establishment or commit other crimes. Often times when these criminals are caught, they provide false identification implicating you. If these are minor crimes like misdemeanors, they can go on your criminal record without your knowledge. However, if the crime is more serious, law enforcement officials can take you to jail. Then, you may have to hire a lawyer to help sort everything out. So save yourself the hassle: Get a copy of your criminal report from your local police station periodically to make sure no one has committed crimes using your name.

Protection for Internet Purchases

Because identity theft is costing businesses more than $50 billion annually, many are working on solutions for reducing losses. CitiGroup now has a free product for its cardholders that allows them to make purchases without giving their actual card numbers. The system generates a random credit card number to make it difficult to steal account information when doing online transactions. Each time you make a purchase on the Internet, a substitute account number is produced, but the purchases are still charged to you and appear on your monthly statement.

Verified by Visa is another program designed to protect consumers making online purchases. When shopping at participating retailers, you would enter the usual information like your name, address, phone number and credit card number. Then, a screen appears asking for a password. This is an added level of protection in case your card or number is stolen. The government is also doing its part by imposing stiffer penalties for identity theft cases. Individuals convicted of non-terrorist identity theft will receive two-year prison sentences.

Phishing/Spoof E-mails

The origin of the word phishing comes from the analogy that imposters are using e-mail lures to "fish" for personal and account information. "Ph" is a common replacement for "f" by hackers. Phishing e-mails (also known as spoof e-mails) are designed to direct you to another Web site with the goal of stealing your personal identification or account information to commit fraud.

Phishers use clever tactics by pretending to be well-known companies such as banks and Internet merchants to gain your trust so that you will visit their Web sites. A few examples of some popular phishing e-mails are provided below. If you see these or similar ones directing you to another Web site, do not click on the link within the e-mail. Be sure to read the Internet address. Someone claiming to be Bank of America might direct you to a site other than its actual address (www.bankofamerica.com).

Tips to spot Phishing e-mails

Urgent appeals – These e-mails may claim that your account will be closed if you fail to confirm your personal information immediately.

Request for Security Information – Occasionally, phishing e-mails may suggest your financial institution has lost important information and needs an update.

Typos or other errors – Often times these e-mails have spelling or grammatical errors. In addition, there may be a message at the bottom of the e-mail that has nothing to do with the main content.

Sample lines

Below are a few examples of e-mail subject headers that can alert you to a possible phisher:

"Unusual login attempts to your personal account"
"Your account has been violated"
"Important Account Information"
"Valued Customer"

Phone Phishers

Phishers try to lure people on the telephone too. Some may call you claiming to be employees of credit card companies and ask for the three digit security code on the back of your card. Even if these scammers have your account number, they may not be able to rack up charges unless they have this code. Merchants use it to verify the card belongs to you when you make transactions on the Internet or telephone. Only give this sensitive information out to sources you're sure are legitimate. If you are not on the National Do Not Call Registry, sign up at www.donotcall.gov to limit calls from telemarketers. You can register your home and cell phone numbers.

E-MAIL HOAXES

If you receive an e-mail that claims you can receive a large monetary award for a small fee or asks you to forward that e-mail on to others, it may be a scam. Some of the more common hoaxes are the Nigerian 419, chain letters, and lottery winning e-mails. Check out the examples below.

Nigerian 419 Scam

This type of e-mail requests your help in moving a large sum of money out of Nigeria or some other country. They will ask that you pay some fees in advance before you can receive your windfall. Think about this for a minute, why would they just randomly pick you to help in this transaction when the sender knows nothing about you? Below is one version of the e-mail:

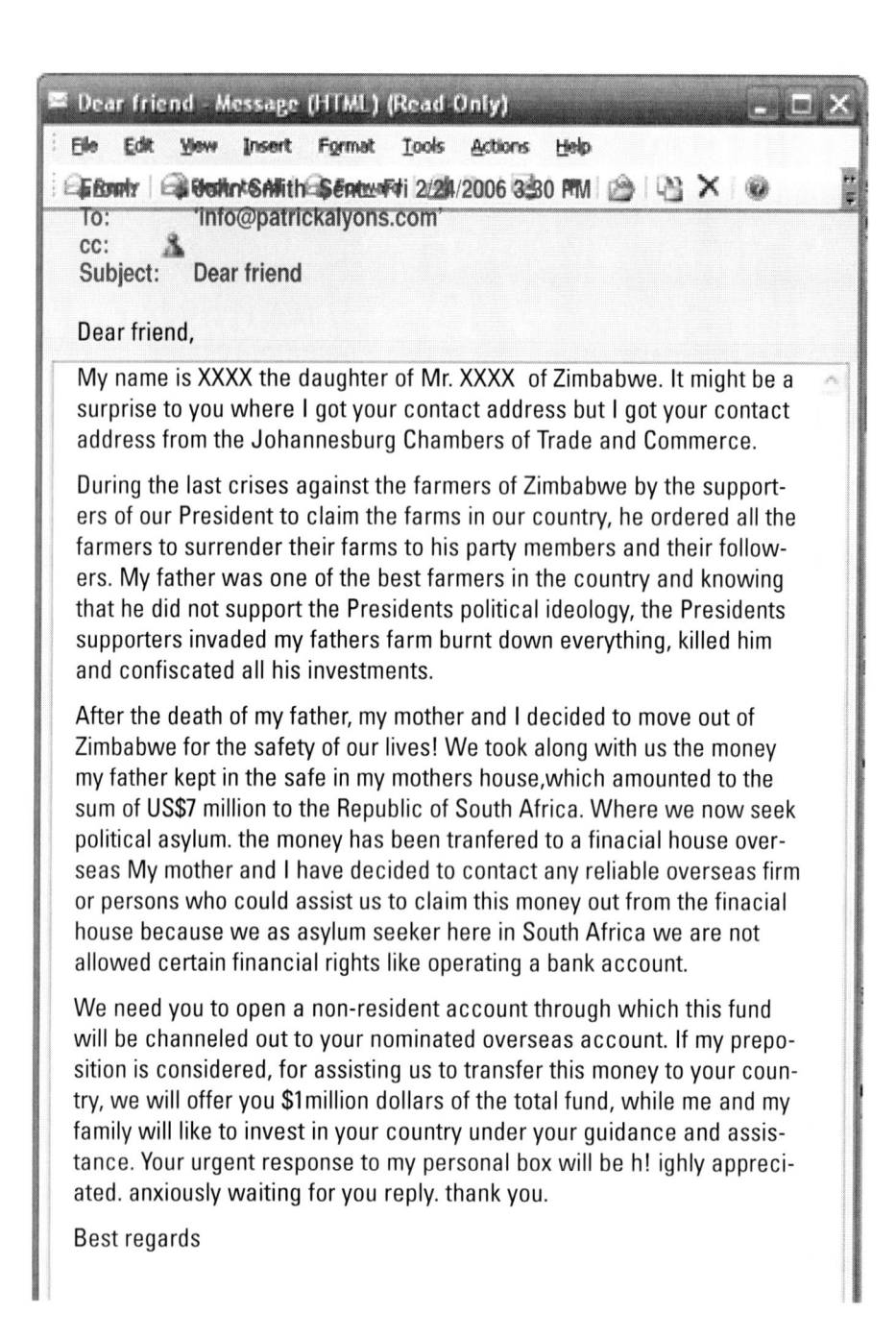

From:	John Smith Sent: Fri 2/24/2006 3:30 PM
To:	'info@patrickalyons.com'
cc:	
Subject:	Dear friend

Dear friend,

My name is XXXX the daughter of Mr. XXXX of Zimbabwe. It might be a surprise to you where I got your contact address but I got your contact address from the Johannesburg Chambers of Trade and Commerce.

During the last crises against the farmers of Zimbabwe by the supporters of our President to claim the farms in our country, he ordered all the farmers to surrender their farms to his party members and their followers. My father was one of the best farmers in the country and knowing that he did not support the Presidents political ideology, the Presidents supporters invaded my fathers farm burnt down everything, killed him and confiscated all his investments.

After the death of my father, my mother and I decided to move out of Zimbabwe for the safety of our lives! We took along with us the money my father kept in the safe in my mothers house,which amounted to the sum of US$7 million to the Republic of South Africa. Where we now seek political asylum. the money has been tranfered to a finacial house overseas My mother and I have decided to contact any reliable overseas firm or persons who could assist us to claim this money out from the finacial house because we as asylum seeker here in South Africa we are not allowed certain financial rights like operating a bank account.

We need you to open a non-resident account through which this fund will be channeled out to your nominated overseas account. If my preposition is considered, for assisting us to transfer this money to your country, we will offer you $1million dollars of the total fund, while me and my family will like to invest in your country under your guidance and assistance. Your urgent response to my personal box will be h! ighly appreciated. anxiously waiting for you reply. thank you.

Best regards

Chain Letters

Chain letters will ask you to forward the e-mail to as many people as possible and visit a particular Web site in hope that someone will fall for the scam and share personal information. Below is one that I received:

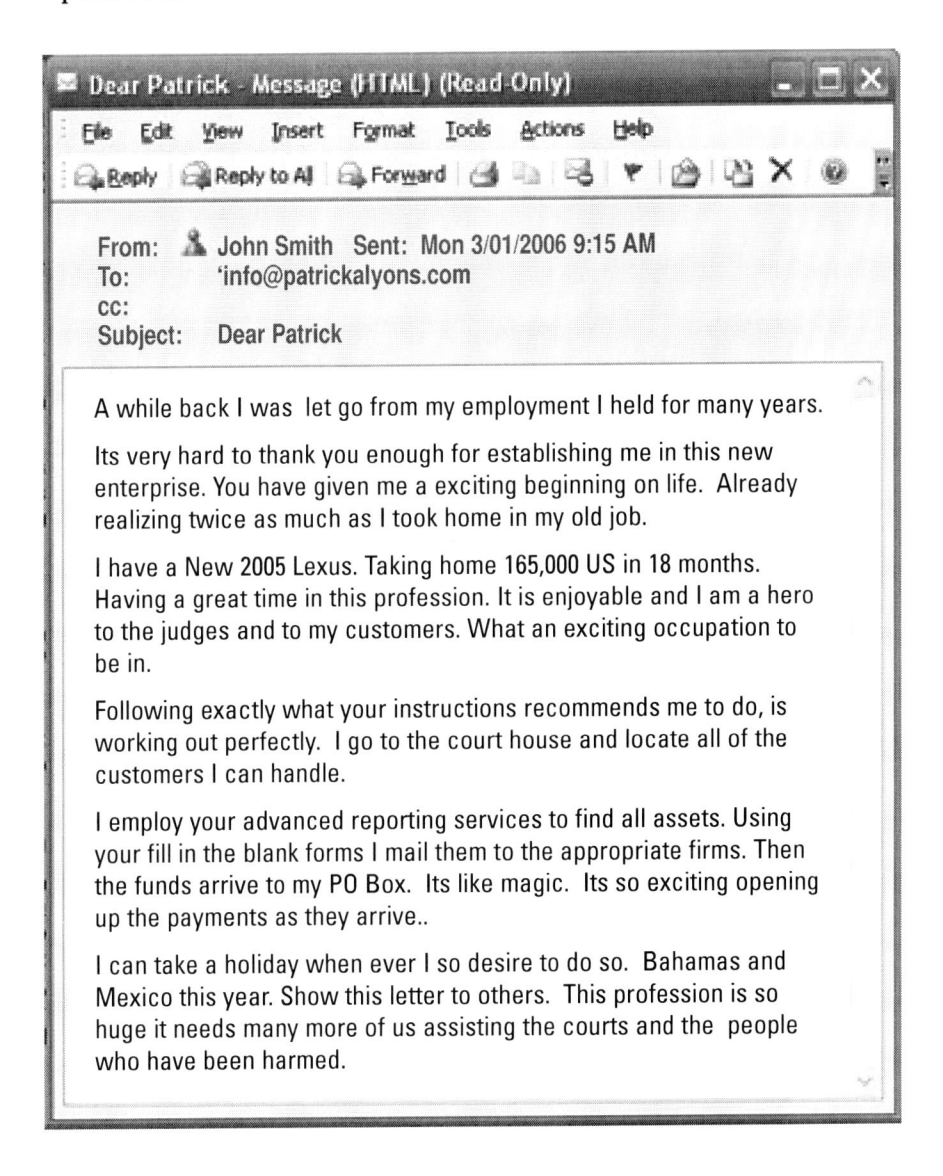

Dear Patrick - Message (HTML) (Read-Only)

From: John Smith   Sent: Mon 3/01/2006 9:15 AM
To: 'info@patrickalyons.com
cc:
Subject: Dear Patrick

A while back I was let go from my employment I held for many years.

Its very hard to thank you enough for establishing me in this new enterprise. You have given me a exciting beginning on life. Already realizing twice as much as I took home in my old job.

I have a New 2005 Lexus. Taking home 165,000 US in 18 months. Having a great time in this profession. It is enjoyable and I am a hero to the judges and to my customers. What an exciting occupation to be in.

Following exactly what your instructions recommends me to do, is working out perfectly. I go to the court house and locate all of the customers I can handle.

I employ your advanced reporting services to find all assets. Using your fill in the blank forms I mail them to the appropriate firms. Then the funds arrive to my PO Box. Its like magic. Its so exciting opening up the payments as they arrive..

I can take a holiday when ever I so desire to do so. Bahamas and Mexico this year. Show this letter to others. This profession is so huge it needs many more of us assisting the courts and the people who have been harmed.

Lottery Scams

These e-mails usually claim that you won some type of international lottery. The phisher will ask you to send a fee to claim it, so think twice if you receive an e-mail claiming you have won a lottery. The following page is one that I received.

Money Laundering

You may receive an e-mail that asks you to process a payment, check or money order. The sender will request that you deposit his or her check into your account and forward the money to them electronically. These checks will often bounce, which can cause your bank to charge you fees. Even more dangerous, the perpetrator can implicate you in the crime if he is caught. So beware this rip off.

For more examples, visit www.hoax-slayer.com and www.antiphishing.org

NOTES

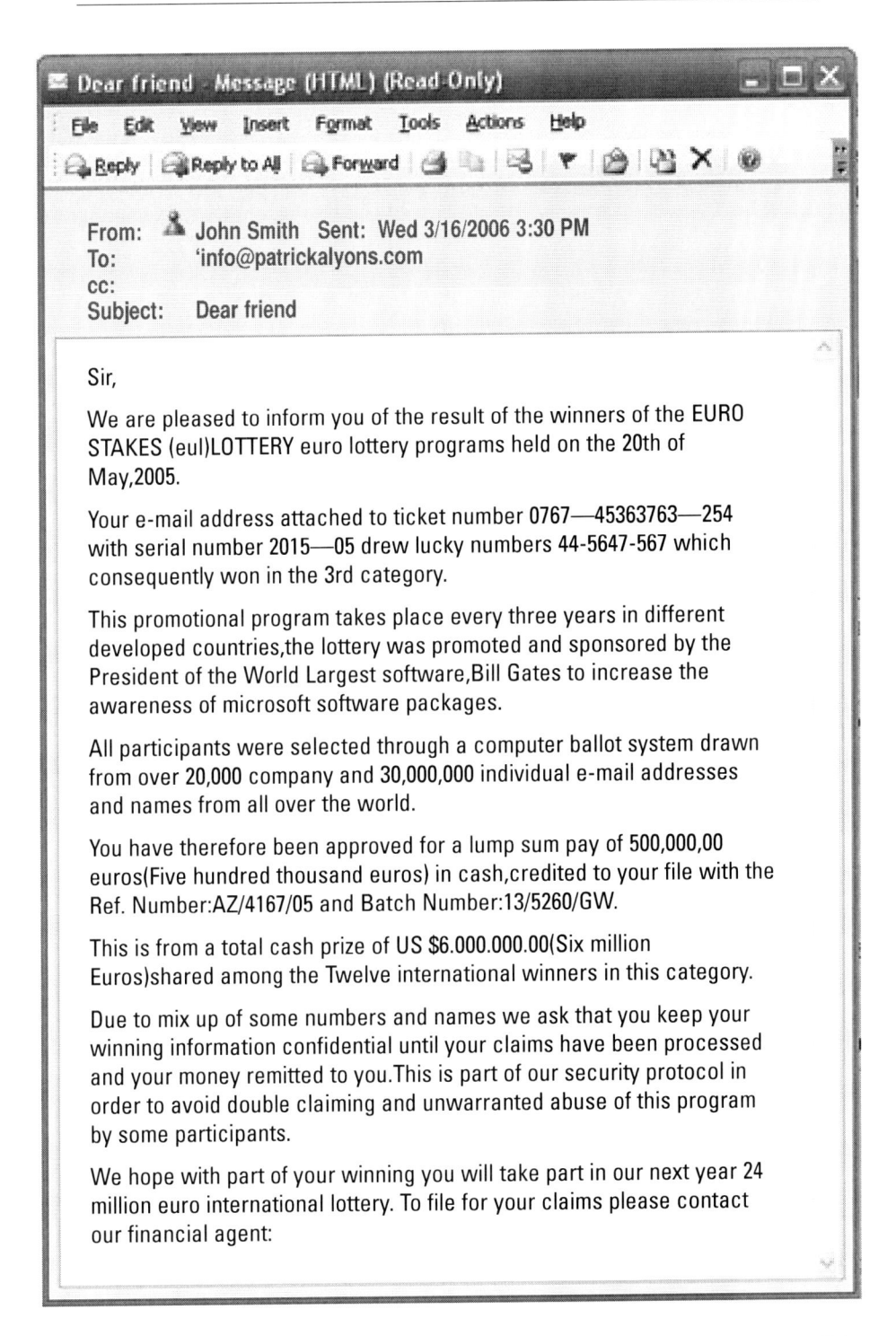

From: John Smith   Sent: Wed 3/16/2006 3:30 PM
To: 'info@patrickalyons.com
cc:
Subject: Dear friend

Sir,

We are pleased to inform you of the result of the winners of the EURO STAKES (eul)LOTTERY euro lottery programs held on the 20th of May, 2005.

Your e-mail address attached to ticket number 0767—45363763—254 with serial number 2015—05 drew lucky numbers 44-5647-567 which consequently won in the 3rd category.

This promotional program takes place every three years in different developed countries,the lottery was promoted and sponsored by the President of the World Largest software,Bill Gates to increase the awareness of microsoft software packages.

All participants were selected through a computer ballot system drawn from over 20,000 company and 30,000,000 individual e-mail addresses and names from all over the world.

You have therefore been approved for a lump sum pay of 500,000,00 euros(Five hundred thousand euros) in cash,credited to your file with the Ref. Number:AZ/4167/05 and Batch Number:13/5260/GW.

This is from a total cash prize of US $6.000.000.00(Six million Euros)shared among the Twelve international winners in this category.

Due to mix up of some numbers and names we ask that you keep your winning information confidential until your claims have been processed and your money remitted to you.This is part of our security protocol in order to avoid double claiming and unwarranted abuse of this program by some participants.

We hope with part of your winning you will take part in our next year 24 million euro international lottery. To file for your claims please contact our financial agent:

Just for Teens

1 As a teenager, you are a likely target of identity theft. Criminals go after younger people because they think they know less about how people steal account information. Be careful about who you share personal information with. There are few reasons anyone at your school should know your Social Security or driver's license number. If someone requests that information, ask them why they need it before sharing.

2 A lot of consumer electronic devices like iPods and Personal Digital Assistants (PDAs) allow you to store personal information. If you do have sensitive information stored in these devices, make sure you don't leave them lying around. Setting passwords can also prevent information from being stolen.

> Be sure to use passwords that aren't obvious like your name or birthday.

Shortcuts

(Tips to prevent identity theft)

- ☑ Never give out personal account information by e-mail or over the phone.

- ☑ Do not click on links in unsolicited e-mails. There is a good chance it is directing you to a Web site that is collecting personal information.

- ☑ Keep your passwords to yourself and memorize them. When creating your passwords, avoid obvious choices like your name, birthday or pet's name. Do not carry them in your wallet or purse.

- ☑ Be sure to sign off Web sites instead of just closing your browser. This is especially important if you are using a computer open to the public because someone could access your information after you leave.

- ☑ Never leave receipts at ATMs. Take them home and shred them immediately.

- ☑ When using ATMs, be aware of your surroundings. If you feel wary, cancel your transaction and leave immediately. Try to avoid using ATMs at night because someone could easily sneak up on you.

PART 3

≫ The Pit Stop

CHAPTER 7

» Defining Financial Freedom

Some people bring home $24,000 a year and are free from debt, while others earn $150,000 a year and live paycheck to paycheck.

Achieving financial freedom has little to do with your salary. Making more money doesn't always make you happy. But what can give you peace of mind is having a plan to achieve your financial goals. Use the tools outlined earlier in the book on budgeting and managing credit wisely. Also create a disciplined savings plan and find a job you enjoy. In this chapter, we will explore ways of discovering the right career for you.

Finding Your Dream Job

Searching for a job requires a lot of effort. The days of working for one company your whole career are over. Some people may switch jobs once or twice, while others labor their whole life and never find their perfect job. But once you find one that allows you to pursue your passion, the journey becomes worthwhile. Coming to work brings fulfillment and peace when you are doing something you enjoy.

Assessing your career

Before even starting your job search, determine your interests. One way to do that is by taking a personality test. There are several types you can try. The Keirsey Temperament Sorter II and the Jung-Myers-Briggs Typology Test are among the most popular ones. Don't let the names scare you. They sound complicated, but they're really simple surveys that can help you learn more about yourself and figure out what career path to choose. You can take the Keirsey Temperament Sorter II for free by visiting www.keirsey.com. There is also a free test based on the Jung-Myers Briggs approach at www.humanmetrics.com.

Creating a resume

After you zero in on your interests, create a resume to help you get the job you want. List your responsibilities from previous jobs and highlight your achievements. Tell the truth. Lying about qualifications and exaggerating accomplishments can get you fired.

Think of legitimate ways to make your resume stand out. Choose a well-designed style that fits your career choice and personality. Write with strong verbs. Check for typos, spacing and grammatical errors. That's the best way to make a good impression.

You may have heard that resumes have to be just one page long. Some experts say two pages are fine as long as the information is related to the position you're seeking.

Looking for Jobs

Internet

With the growth of the Internet, looking online for a job has become a cheap and efficient way of finding work. Sites like Monster.com and Careerbuilder.com allow users to post resumes and apply for positions. These sites are both a resource for high school and college students searching for summer jobs and internships and working adults looking for full- and part-time jobs. Unlike snail mail, which can take days to reach employers, a resume posted on the Internet can land there with the click of a button.

Another helpful feature of job Web sites are their resources. Many provide tips to prepare candidates for interviews and give background information on the companies positing jobs. These extras can give you the competitive advantage you need to edge out the competition.

Networking

What is networking? It's meeting people, exchanging ideas and information, forging professional and personal connections. You can make formal contacts through professional and trade organizations. These groups often hold meetings or social gatherings where you can interact and exchange business cards. Informal contacts can come from friends, family and neighbors. You can also create these ties by volunteering. You may meet someone who works at the company at which you wish to apply.

When networking, you can ask contacts for direct job leads or ask them for information and advice that can help in your job search. Several companies fill jobs by getting employee referrals, so if there is a place you are interested in, make contact with someone in the department you would like to work. Offer to take that person to lunch or set up a time to go by his or her office to sell your skills. That way when an opening becomes available, they may think of you and give you a call.

Newspapers

Although more employers are listing jobs on the Internet, newspapers are still a good source of job openings. The Sunday paper is a great place to check out listings if you are limiting your search to a specific geographic region.

Companies

Some companies prefer to recruit the old-fashioned way rather than open themselves up to the volume of resumes that may come with posting openings on the Internet. But even if a company has no advertised vacancy, you can still send your resume. Find out the name of the manager in the department you wish to work for and schedule an informational interview to highlight your strengths. This type of initiative can put you at the top of the list of candidates when a job becomes available.

Search Firms

Search firms, also known as headhunters or recruiters, can be a useful source for job openings. Companies use these firms to screen job candidates and narrow the list for interviews rather than having to pour over hundreds or thousands of resumes to find qualified applicants for certain specialized jobs. You may apply for a job over the Internet and find that the job was posted by a search firm. Headhunters also network to find candidates. But remember the goal of a headhunter is to get you to accept a job. He or she could care less whether it is a good fit for you. Once you take the job, the headhunter receives a commission.

Thank You

After interviews, remember to send thank you notes. Mail them within two days of your meeting. Some say it is fine to send an email for a thank you, but I would suggest a typed or handwritten note. Since Internet service providers are using spam blockers, your thank you email may not reach the person if you are not in his or her address book. Plus, giving a personal touch may set you apart from the competition.

Internships

Internships are short-term positions that provide an opportunity to "try out" a job you have an interest in pursuing. I was in Navy ROTC in college. Part of the requirements for being in the program was to participate in summer training. I talked with some Naval officers who served on submarines and they shared how much fun it was traveling around the world, so I requested to be on a submarine for my summer apprenticeship. I was assigned to the USS Lapon (It has since been taken out of service). The food was great, but I didn't enjoy being under water for a month so a career as a submariner was not in the cards for me.

The next year I joined INROADS, which is an organization that helps prepare people of color for jobs in the corporate world by providing workshops and internships to high school and college students. I interned in the trust department of a bank and watched analysts who evaluated stocks prior to buying them for clients. One of the senior officers served as my mentor. We had lunch once a month to discuss my experiences. He was always available to answer any questions. The next summer I returned and worked with portfolio managers, who picked stocks from the analysts' recommendations to construct a diversified portfolio for clients. I learned about the thought process involved in building a portfolio for clients with different needs. I had a chance to see how investments are chosen for the elderly as well as a young person who had won the Florida lottery. I knew after this experience that I wanted to be a portfolio manager, the job I hold today.

Through my internship experiences, I discovered how to use several investment software programs, which helped me land a full-time job after college. Once working, I had a lot to learn, but it didn't take me long to get up to speed because I gained valuable practical experience on my internships.

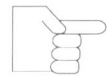

Some sources for internships include:

- **MonsterTRAK** – www.monstertrak.com is a Web site sponsored by Monster.com
- **INROADS** – www.inroads.org
- **InternWeb** – www.internweb.com
- **College Placement offices**
- **Career Fairs**

Understanding Employee Benefits

Did you know companies give employees benefits for coming to work every day? Remember to consider these perks as you evaluate the offers companies make. It depends on what you value most, but in some cases, a generous collection of benefits can make a job with a low-to-average salary more appealing just as a stingy package can cut down the allure of a high salary. Here are some of the most common benefits employers provide:

Paid Time Off

Paid time off is one of the most common benefits offered. It can come in the form of vacation time, which can be used at your discretion, sick time or personal time, which gives you time to handle personal chores. Most companies also give employees various holidays off with pay.

Tuition Reimbursement

Some companies will pay for you to continue your education if it is related to your field of work. These firms typically require you to pay for the cost of tuition and books up front. If you make a passing grade or the grade the company stipulates, they will reimburse you.

Insurance

Insurance is a contract that provides coverage against loss. Policies can be purchased for different contingencies such as loss of life (life insurance), sickness (health insurance) or long-term illness (disability insurance). Companies often offer these benefits at group rates, which are lower than you might be able to get on your own. Some employers will pay your premium. Others may contribute to the cost. Still others will pay nothing at all.

Health Insurance

This insurance helps defray costs if you need to go to the doctor or have other medical needs such as prescription medications. Companies often offer a couple of different types of coverage. One option may provide a lower premium, but require you to pay a higher percentage of your medical costs. The two major types of insurance plans are indemnity and managed care.

Indemnity – Also known as a reimbursement plan, indemnity reimburses you for medical expenses regardless of the provider you choose. In most cases, you will receive a percentage of the costs, not the total amount.

Managed care - This plan comes in two varieties: Health Maintenance Organizations (HMO) and Preferred Provider Organizations (PPO). With HMOs, you select a primary care physician to handle your health-related needs within a set network of doctors. If you need to see a specialist, your doctor will refer you to one within the group. Under HMOS, if you see a doctor who is not covered by your insurance plan, you will pay a significant part of the charges. PPOs provide more flexibility. You don't have to get referrals from a primary care doctor to see specialists and they typically have a larger selection of physicians to choose from.

Disability

If you become so ill you can't work, how will you pay the bills? One solution is having disability insurance, which is offered in some benefit packages. You can receive short-term disability coverage, which will pay a portion of your wages for a specific time period, usually less than two years. For longer lasting health problems, you can purchase a long-term disability insurance policy.

Life Insurance

Life insurance will pay a beneficiary you designate a specific amount of money in the event of your death.

Term versus Whole Life

Term life insurance is a temporary insurance policy. You own it for a specific time period. The duration can range from 10 to 30 years. Once the term is over, you have to renew the policy if you still want coverage. Because you'll be older, it will cost you more. Another drawback of term insurance is that if you are ever late with a premium payment, the policy will lapse and you will have to get a new policy, which may cause your premiums to increase because you are older than when you initially signed up. What draws many people to term insurance is that it's typically cheaper than a whole life policy. The payments are fixed for the life of the policy, in most cases. A 25-year-old nonsmoker in good health, for instance, could buy a $100,000 20-year term policy for as low as $10 a month. Whole life insurance might cost that same person $80 a month.

Whole life insurance is a permanent policy. A portion of your premium goes toward paying a death benefit to your beneficiaries. The rest is placed in an investment account that will be invested in stocks, bonds or both. You generate a cash value from the investment portion of the account, which you can use to withdraw if you ever have an emergency and need cash to avoid using loans. The downside is the policy costs more than term and you have no control over the investment options, which are sometimes very conservative and generate minimal returns. You could purchase a term policy and invest the difference from what you would have paid for a whole life policy in a brokerage account and pick your own investment choices.

So which insurance is best? It depends. A younger person may choose a term policy because the premium is cheaper. If the savings between term and whole life monthly premiums is invested in stocks or mutual funds, it could generate enough wealth to provide for your family in case you have an untimely death. As you become older, the gap in pricing between whole and term life narrows and you may decide to opt for a permanent insurance policy.

Retirement

Some companies offer a variety of retirement saving options. The more common types are 401(k), 403(b) and pension plans, which will be discussed in Chapter 12.

Taxes

I felt great when I received my first paycheck. I was 16 and making $3.35 per hour. I thought that I could multiply my hourly rate by the number of hours I worked to determine how much my paycheck would be. Unfortunately, I didn't realize that Uncle Sam would be getting a hunk of my money. Certain taxes and deductions are subtracted from your paycheck before you receive one penny. They include:

Federal Insurance Contributions Act tax (FICA) - This incorporates Social Security and medicare taxes. Social Security is a program in the United States that gives certain benefits to older Americans such as a retirement check. Each year that you pay a Social Security tax, the Social Security Administration sends a benefit statement showing what you paid and what your projected benefits are. Social Security and Medicare are 6.2% and 1.45% of your gross wages (Employers match those amounts).

Federal Withholding Tax – This is the amount of federal income tax that comes out of your check and is paid to the government. It is based on your filing status (e.g. single, married) and the number of allowances you are withholding. For example, if you are married with no children you can claim two allowances, one for yourself and one for your spouse. Your employer then uses this information to determine how much tax to deduct from each of your paychecks. If your parents can claim you on their tax return it would be zero allowances.

State/Local Income Tax – Several state and local governments charge income tax to fund operations. States such as Alaska, Florida, Nevada, South Dakota, Texas, Washington and Wyoming have no state income taxes.

Just for Teens

If you are under the age of 18 and are seeking employment, check out the child labor laws that govern the state where you live. You may not be able to do certain jobs. Also, there are restrictions on the number of hours you can work during the school year.

Shortcuts

- ☑ Consider taking a personality test. They are great resources that can help you figure out what type of career is right for you.

- ☑ Line up internships. They give you a taste of the working world and a chance to "try out" the job to see if you like it.

- ☑ Search creatively. There are many ways to look for a new job — the Internet, newspapers, networking and search firms. Try them all. If you don't see a listing, dare to take a chance. Apply directly to the company you are interested in working for.

- ☑ Be patient and positive. Finding the perfect job takes time. You may receive several rejection letters before landing the right job. But each one just brings you closer to the perfect career for you.

CHAPTER 8

> **≫ Starting a Business**

Some people would rather work for someone else. But if you have a vision for creating a business of your own, dare to follow your dream.

The Entrepreneur

A successful entrepreneur is one who is self-motivated and has a vision to create something bigger than him or her. As an owner you should be willing to take risks even if it means your business fails. You may stumble with the first venture. But maybe your next one will be the winner or the next. It takes perseverance, grit and humility to work on your goal and grow from your mistakes. But if you stay true to your mission, owning a business can be a rewarding experience with unlimited potential.

Passion

Being an entrepreneur brings challenges, but having passion for your business makes the hardships worthwhile. When you enjoy what you are doing, you worry less about the money you are making. Your primary focus becomes doing the best job you can. When I was 12, too young to apply for a traditional part-time job, my older brother and I started a yard maintenance business. Our dad told neighbors about our service and we landed our first clients through his referrals.

I remember he would come with my brother and me to some of the yards we serviced. If we missed even a blade of grass, he would point it out and make sure we cut it. At the time, I thought, "What does it matter if one piece of grass is taller than the rest?" But when I reached adulthood, I understood his message: When you're running a business, the work you do says a great deal about you. If you want to be seen as an entrepreneur with integrity, you must deliver a quality product. That single blade of grass meant the job was not done.

Other neighbors took notice of the good work we did and we soon garnered more business. We started out with one client, but by the end of the summer we had five, which was all we cared to handle because we wanted time to enjoy our summer break from school.

My dad's lesson stayed with me: Be professional, even if you are working with family and friends. If you say you are going to perform a job at a certain time, keep your word. Give your customers the kind of service you would like to receive. It shows how sincere you are and how much pride you take in your work.

Business Plan

In the first chapter, I gave an acronym for the word PRIDE. The P stands for preparation and that's what a business plan is, laying the groundwork for how you're going to run your venture. Being successful requires preparation and hard work.

Business plans are often used to help entrepreneurs win money from outside investors or secure loans from banks. However, they are also a blueprint for your business. They make you think about what product or service you plan to offer and how you will deliver it to your target market. A well-written business plan will help you grow your business because it includes fundamentals like your mission statement, marketing plan and goals.

Lengths of business plans vary. It may start out as a five-page document, but as your business progresses, it could turn into a 50-page report. Some simple business concepts can be explained in a few words. But if you're selling a highly technical product, it may take several pages to describe. Write as much as you need to cover the bases.

If you want to use the plan to raise money from potential investors, write clearly and thoroughly explain all of your products or services without too much technical jargon. If not, you may lose potential investors who are unwilling to take on a product they don't understand. There are many variations of business plans. Here are some of the major elements:

Executive Summary

This section appears first in a business plan, but should be written after all the other parts have been completed. It gives a short rundown of what the entire proposal is about. This summary is your first – and

101

perhaps only chance – to win the interest of investors. If it fails to catch their attention, they may not read the rest of your business plan.

Company Overview

Here, you provide a history of your firm. Include information such as the date your firm was founded, a discussion of your business strengths and a mission statement that explains why you are starting this venture. Below is a sample mission statement:

Joe's mobile detailing business was founded to accommodate busy professionals who want to have their vehicles cleaned on a regular basis, but have no time in their busy schedules to wait at a car wash. We go to the homes or businesses of our clients to provide a quality exterior and interior cleaning of their vehicles at a reasonable price.

Product Overview

Use this area to share information about the product or service you are going to offer. What are the benefits? Why is it needed now? If you are starting a tutoring business, for example, the benefit to clients could be increased understanding of subject matter, which could lead to a better grade in a class. In the product overview section, it is also important to explain what makes your product different from the competition.

Marketing Plan

The marketing plan is a crucial part of any business plan. It lays out your strategy for getting new clients. There are many approaches you can use. You can make presentations, pass out fliers, collect referrals from satisfied customers. The marketing plan also spells out your target market.

Do research to find out if your product is needed in the marketplace. A lot of times, inventors figure they just have to build something wonderful and people will flock to buy it. Before spending too much time and money, determine whether there is a market that may benefit from your product or whether something similar is already available. Doing your homework also involves checking out the competition. Talk to customers of rival companies to find out what they like or dislike about a particular product. Also ask what features they would like to see.

Market research can also be useful in determining a price for your product. Ask potential customers how much they would be willing to pay. If the product or service is more expensive than the competition, you should have some rationale as to why potential customers would pay more for yours.

Set goals for growing your firm. They should be measurable and realistic. For example, a tutor may seek to add 20 clients per month. That's something that can be gauged. He or she may find that getting that many clients at first may be too ambitious. Sometimes it takes a while to establish a customer base. If you are consistently falling short of goals, you may need to adjust them.

Management

This section includes background on the people running your company. If you create a web design business, you may note how many years you have been making web pages and if you took any related course work or have relevant credentials. If you have any advisers who are helping you, mention them too.

Finding a mentor who has experience with the type of product or service you are offering helps you and looks good. An adviser can serve as a sounding board to let you know the pros and cons of a particular field and offer tips. And to outside investors, having a mentor shows that although you may not have a lot of experience in a particular area, you have sought someone who does to guide you as your business grows.

Operational Plan/Milestones

Here, you will describe how your product or service will be produced. You will also detail what supplies and equipment you need. Discuss how many people you require to work at your company and what their functions will be.

Financial Projections

Financial projections, an estimate of your income and expenses, matter to potential investors because they want to invest in businesses where they are likely to make their money back plus get a profit. Smart investors know that most new businesses struggle to break even in the early years, but they expect some type of return on their money down the line.

Many businesses fail because of lack of funding. So when you're estimating your cash needs, add some padding that gives you more money than you think you need to help pay the bills in the beginning while you build a client base.

Final Details

After you write your plan, it's a good idea to have another set of eyes review it to make sure you did not forget any important details. If you can't find someone, find out if your city has a Service Corps of Retired Executives (SCORE). The volunteers are men and women who have spent several years either working for corporations or running their own firms. They've joined SCORE to offer advice to new and existing business owners. They offer free counseling sessions and provide low-cost workshops on topics such as starting a business and writing a business plan. When you launch a business, there are going to be some areas where you lack expertise. You may have a creative mind and conceive innovative products, but lack the financial know-how to run a business. Organizations like SCORE and the Entrepreneurs' Organization can provide guidance in areas where you need help.

Family, Friends & Business

When starting a business, it's natural to ask your family and friends for help. Treat them with the same level of professionalism you would show any investor or customer. Draw up written agreements outlining how you will be using the resources they provide. If you borrow money, set up a payment schedule and be sure to pay the bill on time. If a friend or relative offers consulting services, be sure to spell out in a contract or letter agreement what service your friend is providing and what compensation will be paid. Failing to show respect and fairness in your business dealings with loved ones can strain relationships.

Just for Teens

If you have a creative mind and a strong work ethic, you can turn almost any idea into a business opportunity. Here are a few possibilities:

1 Car Wash

Adults are busy and many put off doing chores. Consider starting a mobile car wash business where you go to your customers' homes to wash and vacuum their vehicles. Many people are willing to pay for the convenience of having their car cleaned at their house rather than doing it on their own or waiting in line to do it somewhere else.

2 Pet Sitting

If you love animals, a pet walking/sitting business may be a cool job for you. Americans spend lots of money on their pets each year. Some people may want someone who is willing to walk their dog on a daily basis. Others may want a pet sitter when they are going out of town and can't travel with the pet. Come up with a list of services and prices tailored to different situations.

3 Tutoring

If there is a subject you get high grades in, consider becoming a tutor. I was a math major in college. When I realized that many students struggle with that subject, I turned offering math help into a business.

4 Personal Shopper

A lot of people dislike shopping for gifts. Others just don't have the time. That's where you can come in. Enjoy the mall? Department stores? What if you had a chance to shop and get paid?

Personal shoppers create a profile of the person they are shopping for and then put their creativity to work as they look for exciting gifts. Another type of personal shopper does grocery shopping. Along with busy professionals, elderly and disabled people may be potential clients.

5 Lawn Maintenance

Many people are willing to pay someone to mow the lawn during the spring and summer, rake the leaves in the fall and remove snow in the winter. Time is very important and it is something a price tag can't be placed on. It takes a lot of work to maintain a yard and many busy homeowners are more than willing to pay someone else to do the work so that they don't have to.

6 Online business

Launching a business selling products on the Internet is an easy, low cost way to make money. The start-up costs vary, but they can be reasonable. If you own a digital camera, it can be helpful to have a picture of the item you are planning to sell. Some members on eBay and other Internet retail sites like to see a picture of an item

107

before bidding or buying. You can ask friends and relatives to donate items they no longer use.

A note about Internet auctions: If you sell on sites like eBay, I encourage completing all transactions through the platform provided. They have a system by which people list products to be sold and help them receive payment.

eBay also has a number of protective services to shield its members from fraud. (Refer to chapter 6 on ways to prevent fraud and identity theft.) You receive no protection though when you complete a transaction outside of the auction site. So don't fall for bids for your product that seem "too good to be true." I was once offered $900 for a computer I was selling for $300. The following page is an excerpt from the e-mail I received.

7 TEMPORARY MOVING BUSINESS

After a college school year is over, it is a hassle to take belongings back home for the summer only to have to return them in the fall. Two of my college classmates started a business moving students' furniture and personal items into storage. They also delivered them when they returned.

Computer for sale - Message (HTML) (Read...

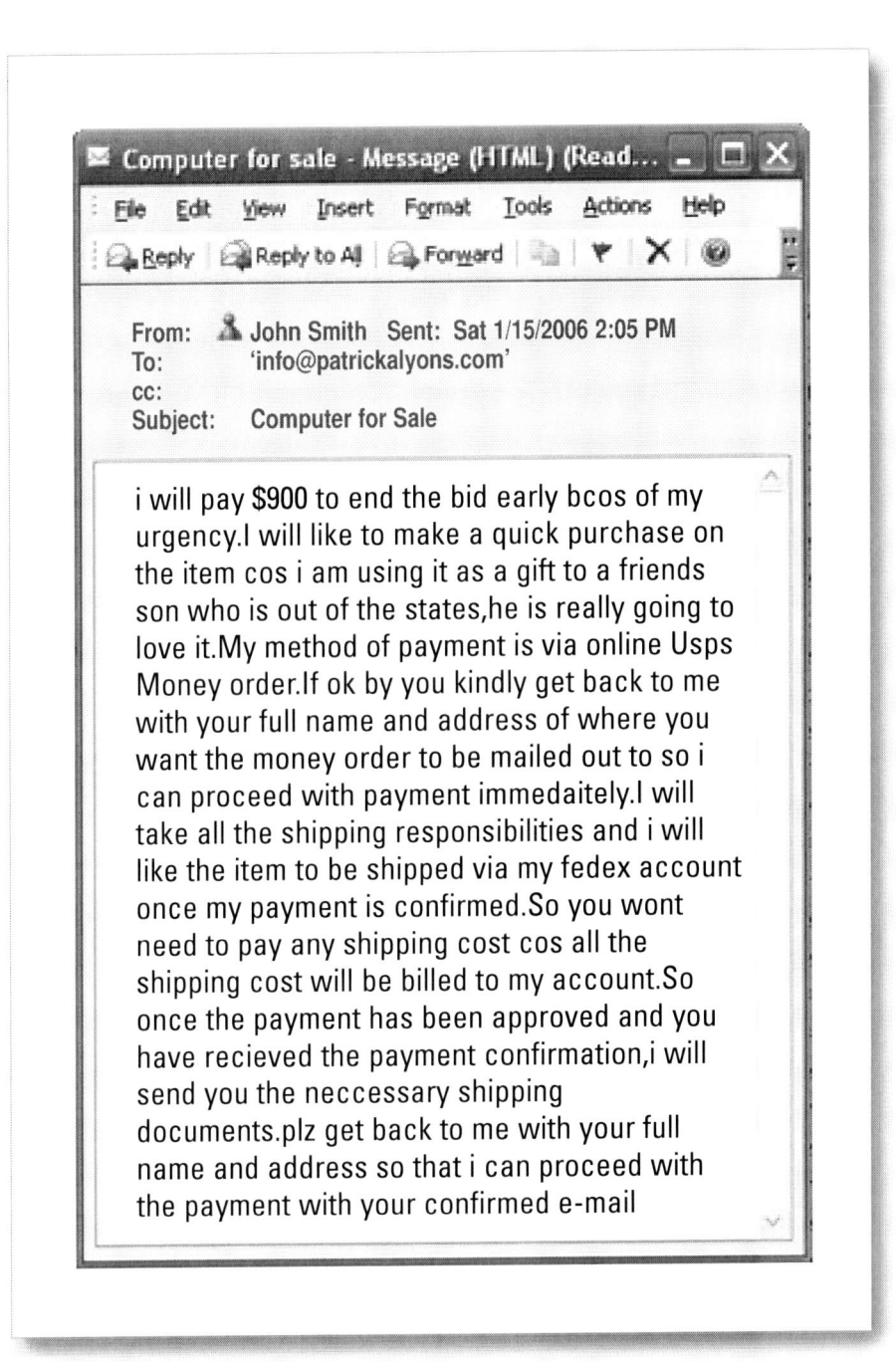

File Edit View Insert Format Tools Actions Help

Reply | Reply to All | Forward

From: John Smith Sent: Sat 1/15/2006 2:05 PM
To: 'info@patrickalyons.com'
cc:
Subject: Computer for Sale

i will pay $900 to end the bid early bcos of my urgency.I will like to make a quick purchase on the item cos i am using it as a gift to a friends son who is out of the states,he is really going to love it.My method of payment is via online Usps Money order.If ok by you kindly get back to me with your full name and address of where you want the money order to be mailed out to so i can proceed with payment immedaitely.I will take all the shipping responsibilities and i will like the item to be shipped via my fedex account once my payment is confirmed.So you wont need to pay any shipping cost cos all the shipping cost will be billed to my account.So once the payment has been approved and you have recieved the payment confirmation,i will send you the neccessary shipping documents.plz get back to me with your full name and address so that i can proceed with the payment with your confirmed e-mail

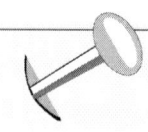

Shortcuts

- ☑ Choose a business you have a passion for. If you do, coming to work won't feel like a chore.

- ☑ Develop a business plan that is realistic. You may want sales to take off right away, but it may take months or even years before your company is making a profit.

- ☑ Ask for help. There are going to be areas where you need assistance, find a mentor to provide advice.

- ☑ Secure funding for your business. Many businesses fail because the owners underestimate how much cash is needed to get it started and keep it going.

PART 4

>> In the Homestretch

CHAPTER 9

> ≫ Education Never Ends

I once thought graduating from college meant the end to taking courses. But I soon found out that education is a never-ending journey.

Continuing Education

To be a contender in your field and to reach your earnings potential, you have to keep learning and growing.

Many jobs today require more advanced skills than a high school education provides. In the investment industry, there are certifications. Highly technical jobs require specialized courses or degrees. Careers in health care and computers may require additional schooling because of advances and developments in the field. Some careers benefit from taking enrichment classes or getting a master's degree or doctorate.

Getting an education does not mean you have to go to a four-year college. Community colleges and vocational schools can prepare you for the demands of the workforce as well. The Census Bureau estimates that between 2002 and 2012 more than 56 million jobs will be created, and people entering the workforce for the first time with a bachelor's or graduate degree will take approximately 14 million of those jobs. That leaves more than 40 million jobs to be filled.

Studies have shown higher education leads to more income. According to the Census Bureau, workers without a high school diploma earned an average salary of $18,734 compared with those with advanced schooling who averaged more than $74,000 per year in 2004.

The higher the education level someone completed, the 2003 Current Population Survey found, the lower the rate of unemployment. The average jobless rate in 2003 was 4.8%. The unemployment rate for individuals with less than a high school diploma was more than 8 percent. It was just 3.3% for those holding a bachelor's degree. The chart on the following page highlights differences in unemployment by education level.

Some say employers prefer more educated employees because they tend to learn faster and can adapt more

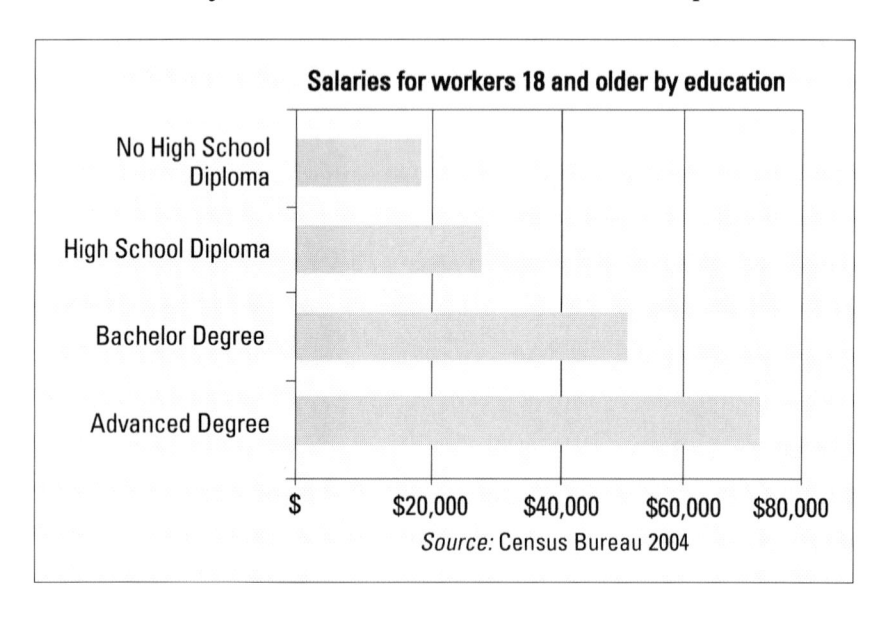

Salaries for workers 18 and older by education

Education	Salary
No High School Diploma	~$18,000
High School Diploma	~$27,000
Bachelor Degree	~$51,000
Advanced Degree	~$74,000

Source: Census Bureau 2004

quickly to change. But it is important to note a bachelor's degree doesn't mean you're exempt from layoffs or that you will automatically make more money than someone with a high school diploma. College graduates are unemployed like everyone else, but having a degree can help you qualify for jobs that are available only to those with a post-secondary education.

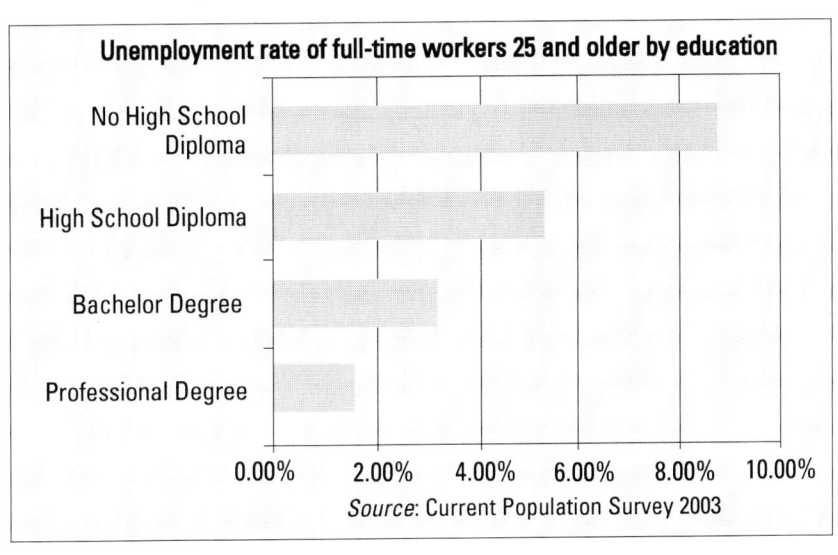

Unemployment rate of full-time workers 25 and older by education

No High School Diploma	~8.5%
High School Diploma	~5%
Bachelor Degree	~3%
Professional Degree	~2%

Source: Current Population Survey 2003

Community College

Community colleges can serve as a bridge between high school and four-year colleges. They also provide the practical skills necessary to work in certain specialized occupations. If you're unsure about attending college full time, these institutions can be a good option. Tuition is cheaper. Associate's degrees and other certifications are awarded, which can be used to upgrade your career. Also, credits you complete at community colleges are often accepted by four-year schools. If you decide to continue your studies and earn a bachelor's degree, you'll already have some of the course work done.

Four-Year Colleges

College tuition costs rise more than 6% every year. That's twice as much as the historical rate of inflation, which is an increase in the prices for goods and services that leads to a decrease in your buying power, for the U.S. economy. According to the College Board, the average cost of private four-year tuition for the 2004-2005 school year is more than $20,000, while public school tuition is more than $5,000. A college education can be expensive, but consider the benefits such as greater earning potential and the opportunity to apply for jobs that are only available to college graduates.

Average 2004 Undergraduate Charges

	Tuition & Fees	Room & Board	Total
4 year private	$20,045.00	$7,420.00	$27,465.00
4 year public	$5,123.00	$6,250.00	$11,373.00

Source: College Board

Education for the Working Adult

Many working adults cannot afford to go back to school full time. They have responsibilities such as caring for family or may lack the financial resources to pay for a heavy course load. Colleges and trade schools realize that attending classes during the day does not work for everyone. Educators are also realizing that face-to-face interactions aren't the only effective means of teaching. Several schools offer flexible options to help working adults continue their education while working full time. Here are a few:

ONLINE EDUCATION

Growing up, I would have never imagined someone could obtain a college degree by taking classes on the Internet.

But today, many schools have web-based education. Online education programs are convenient for people who don't have the time to physically attend school.

There are two types of programs under Internet education — asynchronous and synchronous:

Synchronous (simultaneous) are programs typically conducted online. Students are required to log in at a specified time for class. Instructors often communicate with students by sending instant messages. The benefit of this type of program is that the instructor is available during the scheduled class time to answer any questions you may have. A drawback is that class time could interfere with your other activities.

Asynchronous programs allow students to work at their own pace to complete assignments. Instructors place documents on the Internet which students can review at their convenience. If you are self-motivated and disciplined, asynchronous education is a great option.

With so many online universities emerging, be sure to do your homework. Here are some things to consider when choosing an online school:

- **Is the school accredited?** If so, by whom? Some organizations make up accreditation names to seem credible. Ask the school for contact information and call to speak with someone there. Check out the Council for Higher Education Accreditation (www.chea.org) to find a list of schools that are accredited.
- **Who are the instructors?** Check to see if they are real people. Most Web sites will have faculty e-mail addresses, so send an e-mail or try to contact them by phone. If the school does not list any names and bios, be wary of sending money because it could be a scam.
- **How long has the school been around?** Many disreputable schools such as diploma mills

(discussed below) have only existed for a short period of time. The longer the school has been around, the better.
- **Does the school offer credit for life experience?** Some schools will give credits based on work experience in the military as well as the private sector to help students complete their degrees in a shorter time.

Night & Weekend Programs

If you don't feel comfortable with online classes and would rather sit in a classroom, night and weekend programs may be right for you. I earned my master's degree through night school. I probably could have completed my degree quicker through an online program, but in a classroom setting, I was able to work on skills such as public speaking and working on a team. Just as with the other options, night and weekend programs require lots of discipline. Community and four-year colleges offer degree programs as well as career development classes to help you keep pace with our ever-changing economy. You can pursue a degree or just take one class. Check local colleges to find out more about their offerings.

Hybrid Programs

Hybrid programs mix attending classes and working on your own to complete course work. You may be required to attend class half of the time and receive the remaining instruction through online or paper-and-pencil assignments. These programs are good for those who would like more interaction with instructors than traditional online classes provide.

Diploma Mills

Ever receive an ad saying you can earn a college degree in a couple of weeks? These companies are known as diploma mills. They award degrees with little or no class work. They are not accredited, but claim to offer authentic college degrees for a flat rate. Below are a couple of e-mails I received from diploma mills:

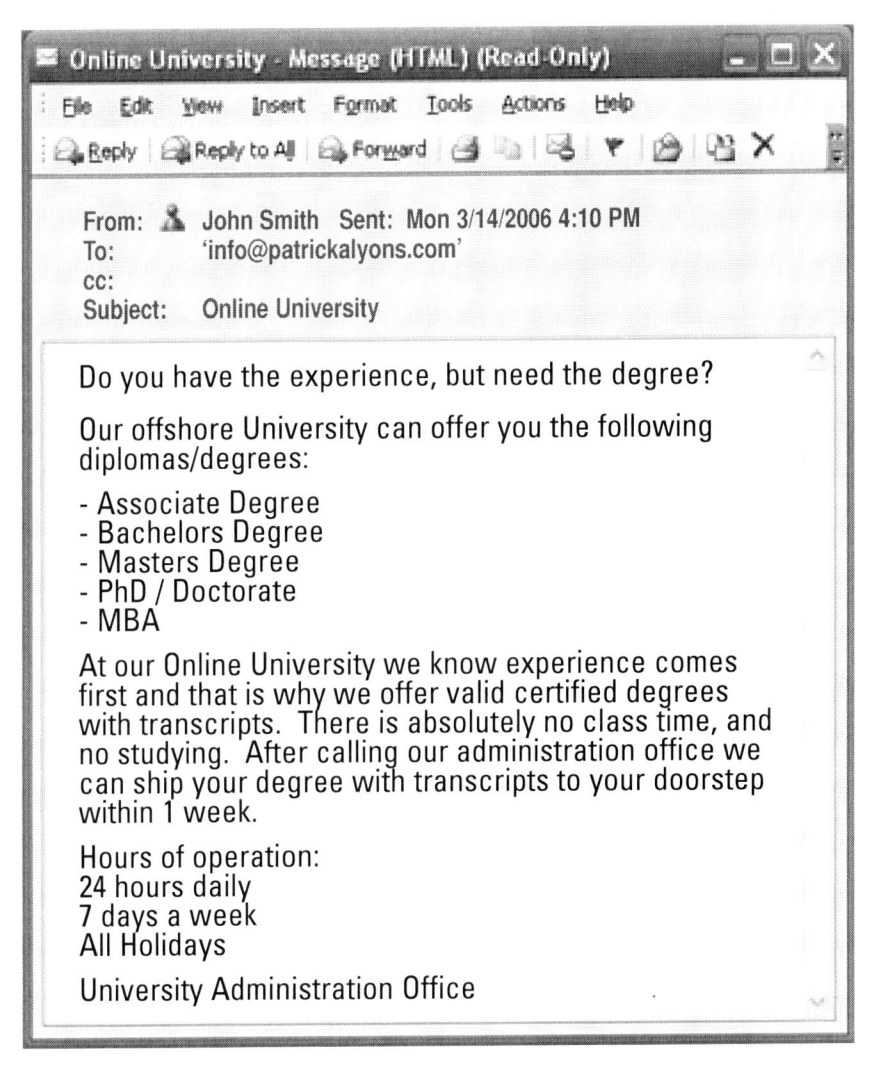

From: John Smith **Sent:** Mon 3/14/2006 4:10 PM
To: 'info@patrickalyons.com'
cc:
Subject: Online University

Do you have the experience, but need the degree?

Our offshore University can offer you the following diplomas/degrees:

- Associate Degree
- Bachelors Degree
- Masters Degree
- PhD / Doctorate
- MBA

At our Online University we know experience comes first and that is why we offer valid certified degrees with transcripts. There is absolutely no class time, and no studying. After calling our administration office we can ship your degree with transcripts to your doorstep within 1 week.

Hours of operation:
24 hours daily
7 days a week
All Holidays

University Administration Office

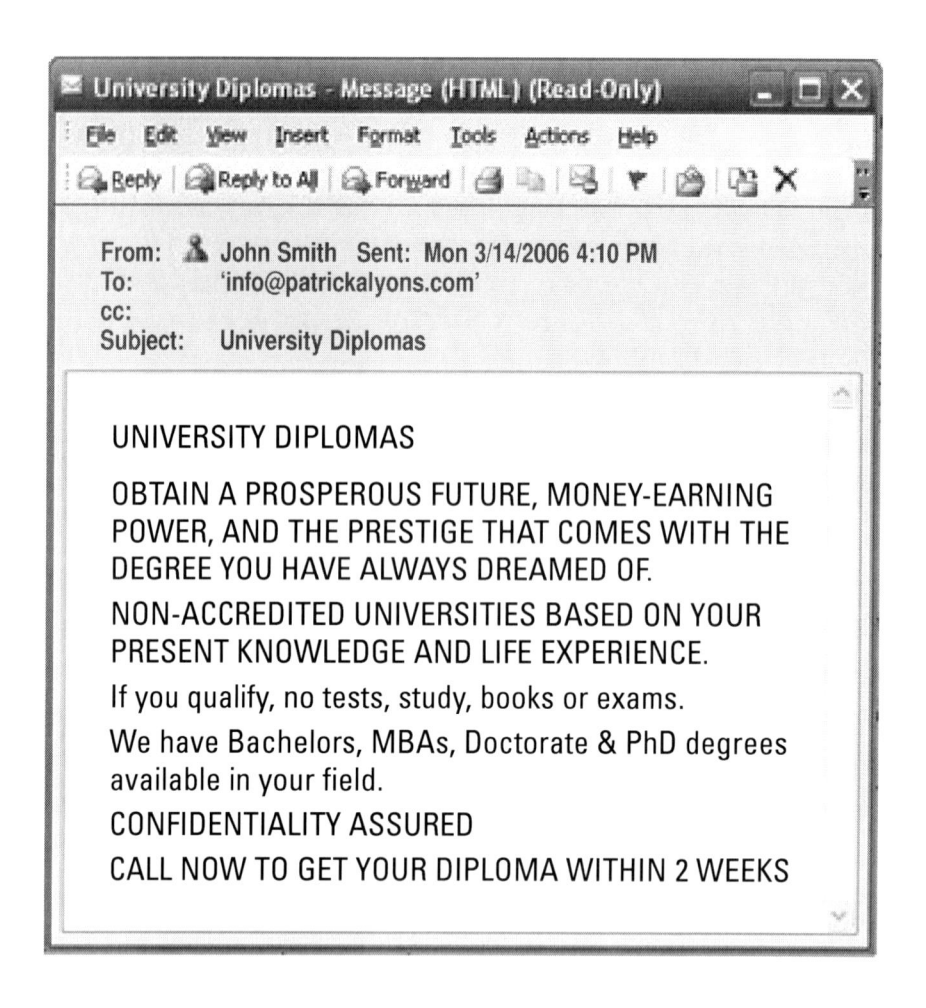

From: John Smith Sent: Mon 3/14/2006 4:10 PM
To: 'info@patricklyons.com'
cc:
Subject: University Diplomas

UNIVERSITY DIPLOMAS

OBTAIN A PROSPEROUS FUTURE, MONEY-EARNING POWER, AND THE PRESTIGE THAT COMES WITH THE DEGREE YOU HAVE ALWAYS DREAMED OF.

NON-ACCREDITED UNIVERSITIES BASED ON YOUR PRESENT KNOWLEDGE AND LIFE EXPERIENCE.

If you qualify, no tests, study, books or exams.

We have Bachelors, MBAs, Doctorate & PhD degrees available in your field.

CONFIDENTIALITY ASSURED

CALL NOW TO GET YOUR DIPLOMA WITHIN 2 WEEKS

Just for Teens

> College can cost a lot, but here are a few ways to reduce the price:

1 If you have reliable transportation, live off campus. I found that the farther I stayed from campus, the cheaper my rent. You may have to cook some meals, but it could end up a lot cheaper than getting the full meal plan on campus.

2 Buy used books. I remember going to purchase a calculus book my freshman year and being told a new one would cost $90, but a used one was only $50. After that, I always bought used textbooks. They had the same information and saved me lots of cash. In addition to being cheaper, you may be able to find useful notes in the margins to aid you in your studies.

3 Consider state schools. The cost of attending a state school can provide a big savings over private schools. Taxpayers fund a significant portion of public school operations so in-state students receive lower tuition as a benefit.

Shortcuts

☑ Continue your education even if you have no plans to earn a college degree. Certain jobs may require you to take a course, get a certification or an advanced degree to win promotions.

☑ Think about attending college. Studies have shown that over the course of their careers, college graduates average higher salaries than their counterparts with high school diplomas.

☑ If you can't attend school full time, consider online schools, night and weekend classes and hybrid programs. Be wary of diploma mills. Many of these organizations will send you a degree for a fee – no courses required. Be sure to research online schools to make sure they're reputable. The longer the school has been around, the less likely it is a diploma mill.

CHAPTER 10

> » Renting and Buying

Are you ready to buy your first home? Should you lease a car? Does renting furniture make sense?

Growing older brings a lot of major decisions. Each choice has its benefits and consequences. You have to decide whether to rent or buy a place to live, or whether to lease or purchase a car. Your selection process will depend on your situation. In this chapter we will explore some things to consider as you make up your mind.

Benefits of renting

MAKES IT EASIER TO MOVE

When you rent an apartment or house, you sign a lease. This is a legal document that requires you to pay

123

for property you occupy for a specific period of time. But there are ways to end your contract early.

I bought a house while I was still renting an apartment. I didn't want to pay rent and a mortgage so I read over my lease to see if there was a way I could get out of it. There was. The cost varies to terminate a lease before your agreed-upon date, but it is possible to leave and keep your good credit rating intact. If you own a home and decide you want to move, you have to sell your house or rent it out. This process can take months to complete.

Offers Lower Move-In Costs

Rental properties usually charge a security deposit. This amount varies by landlord. One apartment manager asked me for a deposit of just $150. Another required me to put up $400. Some places ask for first and last month's rent. If you cause any damage to the apartment, the landlord will use those funds to make repairs so it can be rented again. That may sound like a lot. But if you choose to buy a house you will be paying even more with a down payment. It can be 3% of the purchase price for a loan with the Federal Housing Administration or at least 5% from other sources. You also need cash for closing costs, which can be several thousands more in out-of-pocket funds.

Requires Fewer Monthly Costs

Renting a place to live has lower monthly costs than buying. With a rental, you are not required to purchase homeowner's insurance or pay property taxes but it would be wise to buy renters insurance to protect yourself. Some homeowners also have to pay for mortgage insurance and homeowner association dues.

Closing costs include:

Application fee: This is the charge for applying for a loan. Some banks waive this fee. But it can be $500 or more.

Origination Fee – An amount charged to process your loan.

Private Mortgage Insurance (PMI) – If your down payment is less than 20% of the purchase price, you may be required to get private mortgage insurance. This protects lenders in case you default on your loan

Appraisal Fee – A licensed appraiser will determine the market value of the house you wish to purchase. The fees vary depending on the type and location of the house.

Home Inspection Fee – This is optional, but I would highly recommend you hire an inspector to look for defects prior to completing the purchase. If things are noted before closing, you can require the seller to fix them or lower the price to account for the repairs. Otherwise, he or she risks you walking away.

Credit Report Fee – The charge for the lender running a credit check.

Attorney Fees – This amount covers the cost of an attorney handling the legal paperwork.

Points – Lenders charge points to reduce the interest rate on loans. One point represents 1% of the value of your loan. For example, one point on a $200,000 loan would be $2,000. Paying one point at closing typically reduces the interest rate on a mortgage by 0.25%.

Provides free or low-cost maintenance

If you rent, maintenance staff will fix anything that goes wrong with your apartment for free. If you buy, you're on your own. You can either do it yourself or break out the phone book and your checkbook to find someone to solve your problem. Also, if you rent, you may not have to keep up a yard.

Benefits of owning

Builds net worth

When you rent, you will never own the apartment or house you are leasing unless it is a rent-to-own plan. When you buy, you increase your equity (the difference between the current value of your residence and the amount you owe the bank) as you pay down your mortgage. Real estate prices have historically risen 5% each year, so over time the value of your house will increase.

Offers tax benefits

Mortgage interest and property taxes are deductible on your federal tax return. Points, the amount paid to reduce the interest rate of your loan, are also tax deductible. Another nice benefit is that profits are tax-free up to $250,000 for singles and $500,000 for married couples when you sell your home. That's provided you have owned and lived in the property for at least two years.

Makes costs stable

If you have a fixed-rate mortgage, your payments will be the same for the life of the loan. The property taxes and insurance may change over time, but the amount paid to your lender will not vary. If you rent, you can usually expect to see the bill increase every year.

GIVES YOU FREEDOM

When you own a home, you are free to make any changes you want to the interior of the house. Landlords often will not allow you to make cosmetic changes to rental properties because they want to keep costs down and avoid having to repaint walls, re-tile floors, repair carpet or replace window treatments.

So you want to buy a house?

Buying a house can be an exciting experience, but to make the process go smoothly, we will explore things to work on before shopping for your home.

CREDIT CONSIDERATIONS

Whether you are renting or buying, your credit report will be accessed by either the landlord or bank. If you have credit problems, it will be more difficult to land the place of your dreams.

Having charge-offs and late payments on your credit report will affect the interest rate the bank charges on your mortgage loan. When I got ready to buy my first house, I went to a lender and the loan officer looked at my credit report and saw that I had a few charge-offs and said she could offer me 12% (the national average on a 30-year mortgage at the time was 7%). That meant I would have to pay an extra $500 per month on the house I wanted because of my bad credit.

My real estate agent told me I might be eligible for a Federal Housing Administration loan (FHA), which is a loan made by a private lender but insured by the federal government. Because I had been current on all of my bills for the previous 12 months, I did qualify for the loan. I also had to have enough money for the down payment and sufficient income to pay the mortgage.

As a rule, lenders want to make sure the mortgage payment will be no more than 32% of your income before taxes. They also want to ensure that the mortgage and your other debts do not exceed 41% of your pre-tax income. In short, pay your bills on time. When you do, it helps improve your credit scores, which are used to evaluate your credit worthiness. This makes it easier to buy a house.

Mortgage Brokers

Another option to consider if you have less-than-perfect credit is using a mortgage broker. Some of these firms specialize in helping consumers with bankruptcies and other forms of bad credit buy homes. They have access to many lenders and try to match you with a loan program that meets your needs. It's important to realize if you have a poor credit history, you will pay in the form of high interest rates, fees or both because you are considered a high-risk customer. A mortgage broker has no obligation to get you the best deal. Be sure to ask for a full disclosure of fees. The broker is usually paid an amount for his or her services that may be in addition to what your lender charges. Also, the broker may receive compensation in the form of points added to your loan at closing. If you feel the costs are too high, negotiate something lower or walk away. Knowing the fees up front empowers you by giving you the information you need.

Be sure to get a copy of your credit report prior to applying for a mortgage to verify the information is correct. The last thing you want is to get rejected for a loan because of wrong information in your credit file. If you have late payments noted on your credit report within the last 12 months, you may want to put off buying a house. The cost of a high interest rate may make that perfect home too expensive.

TYPES OF LOANS

Fixed rate

A fixed-rate mortgage is one in which the payment does not change for the life of the loan. Lenders offer 15- and 30-year fixed mortgages. A 15-year mortgage will allow you to pay off the mortgage faster, but will require a higher monthly payment than one for 30 years.

Adjustable rate

Adjustable rate mortgages come in several varieties. These loans are paid over a 30-year period, but the payments are only fixed for a specific time frame such as one, three, five or seven years. At the time of this printing, the rate on a 30-year fixed mortgage was 5.78%. The rate was 5% on a 3-year adjustable rate mortgage. That means choosing the adjustable rate mortgage would save almost $50 per month over the first three years on a $100,000 loan.

After that, the interest rate would change based on a benchmark like the one-year U.S. Treasury bill. When the mortgage rate adjusts, it generally can go up no more than 2% per year, but if your rate went from 5% to 7% on a $100,000 mortgage, your payment would increase by $128 monthly, making your mortgage more expensive.

There is also the chance interest rates would go down, which would lower your payment. The movement of mortgage interest rates is affected by several factors such as the growth of the economy, political events and natural disasters, which are unpredictable.

If you plan to sell your house before the interest rate on your mortgage changes, then it makes sense to get an adjustable rate mortgage. While you're there, you would benefit from the lower interest rate and by moving before the rate changes, you would avoid the risk of a rise in payment. Also remember you can always refinance your adjustable rate loan to a fixed rate at a later date.

Interest-only

Interest-only loans are popular among homebuyers today because you get a low monthly payment, which allows you the opportunity to buy a more expensive house than you could otherwise afford. If you have a $200,000 interest-only mortgage at a 5% annual percentage rate, the payment would be $833 per month versus $1,074 for one that requires principal and interest. It's important to understand that these are 30-year mortgages, but only interest is paid for a set time period (usually less than 15 years). If you pay no principal during that time frame, the amount you owe on the loan would be the same as when you received it. So that $200,000 mortgage you financed would remain $200,000.

When the interest-only period ends, it would be converted to a fully-amortized loan (one that requires principal and interest to be paid). Some of these loans are tied to a fixed rate, but many are adjustable-rate plans where the interest rate is fixed for say five years and can fluctuate thereafter. There are caps that prevent lenders from raising interest rates dramatically in one year, but even a 2% increase would cause payments in the example above to rise from $833 per month to $1,167 (40% more). People who use these loans are gambling that either their income will rise so they can afford to pay for the house at the end of the interest-only period or they anticipate the value of the home increasing in a short time frame so it can be sold at a profit.

An Interest Only Loan May Be Suitable For You If:

- You are buying property to live in or rent, but only plan to own it for a short period of time (five years or less) or
- You will take the difference between the interest-only payment and a fully-amortized loan payment and use it to lower your principal balance or
- You have the investment savvy to pick stocks or some type of high-return vehicle to grow the money in a short period of time.

Be sure to ask if the loan carries a prepayment penalty because if you plan to refinance, you may be hit with a hefty charge. If you are selling your home, prepayment penalties usually don't apply.

PAY EXTRA ON MORTGAGE

Regardless of the type of mortgage you choose, it is always a good idea to pay more than your monthly payment. Any extra you send is applied to the principal balance, which means you will pay for your house faster. If you send an extra $50 per month on a $100,000 30-year fixed mortgage with a 5.75% annual percentage rate, you will pay it off five years sooner and save almost $23,000 in interest costs. If your payment on the loan is $100 more than the stated mortgage, you would pay it off nearly nine years early and you would save more than $37,000 in interest charges.

Some lenders allow for bi-weekly payments (paying half your mortgage payment every two weeks), whereby they make direct debits from your checking account. This method allows you to pay off your loan faster because you are essentially making one extra mortgage payment each year. Using the example above, the loan would be paid off five years early and save nearly $23,000 in interest. You would have to pay the lender or its administrator a fee for the right to participate in this type of program. I would suggest paying an amount above your monthly payment each month because you can do it on your own without paying a charge.

NOTES

BEFORE YOU BUY A HOUSE

☑ **Review a copy of your credit report** – Your credit history plays a major factor in getting approved for a mortgage. Look over your report before you apply for a loan to make sure information is accurate and to avoid any surprises during the application process.

☑ **Get pre-approved** – Once you have your credit in order, go to a bank to get a pre-approval (not to be confused with pre-qualified) letter. The lender will check your credit history and employment information as well as your assets and debts. Then, you will find out the maximum loan value you qualify for. This can be used as a bargaining chip because it shows sellers you can obtain a loan if an offer is made. Some buyers make an offer on a house but cannot qualify for a mortgage.

☑ **Find a real estate agent** – Ask friends and family for recommendations. Another option is to try Homegain (www.homegain.com). Agents compete for your business by presenting proposals on their services. Be sure to interview them to see if they will be able to meet your needs. Find out how long they have been in business. Homegain provides real estate license numbers so you can check whether any complaints have been filed against the agents you are considering. If you have decided on a particular area of town where you wish to buy property, ask the agent how many homes he or she has sold in the area. Someone knowledgeable of the neighborhood can help in determining fair market value when you make an offer on a property.

Leasing versus buying a car

You've probably seen advertisements on TV or in the newspaper that talk about getting a new vehicle for incredibly low monthly payments. They are usually talking about leasing programs. So should you buy or lease? It depends. Here's the deal on each:

BUYING

If you are financing a car through a bank, you usually make a down payment and pay sales taxes. Another cost you will pay is the interest rate the lender charges over the life of the loan. With buying, you can drive your car as much as you wish without having to watch the odometer (with leasing, there are fees if you exceed a certain annual mileage). Another benefit is that after the vehicle is paid for you can lower your insurance limits, which lowers monthly premiums. You also have the option of paying more than what is listed in your installment agreement with the lender which allows you to pay off your loan faster.

When purchasing a vehicle, negotiate the price, not your monthly payment. Some auto lenders will offer you a deal where you pay for your car over eight years to lower your payments, but avoid that if you can. Here's why: It might sound good when a salesman offers you a $20,000 car for $287 a month paid over seven years, especially when you consider that the same vehicle financed for four years, depending on the interest rate, might top $450 a month. But think again. Chances are you will probably trade that vehicle in before you finish paying for it and have negative equity. That means you owe more on the loan than the car is actually worth. If you don't have enough cash to pay off the loan on your old car, the lender will add your other balance to your new vehicle. This creates a never-ending cycle of debt.

Leasing makes sense if you drive less than 15,000 miles per year because that is the typical yearly allowance most companies will permit. If that amount is exceeded, you will pay charges for excess mileage, which can range from $0.10 to $0.25 per mile. I have a friend who went beyond his mileage allowance by 10,000 miles. At the end of his lease term, he owed an extra $1500 or $0.15 per mile. This basically meant he was paying an extra $41.67 each month ($1,500/36) for the lease over his three-year term, which decreased his cost savings by leasing. If you know upfront that you will exceed the mileage, you can pay for extra miles at a reduced rate, but again that reduces your cost savings. Leased vehicles also require a higher level of insurance coverage.

Leasing

With leasing, you pay upfront for a portion of the vehicle's cost and sign on for a short term such as three years. This allows you to have lower monthly payments than you would buying a car and the chance to drive a more expensive car than you might otherwise be able to afford. You will always have a monthly payment with a lease. It is OK to have normal wear and tear, but if there are any damages, you are responsible for the charges. You have three options at the end of a lease contract: You can buy the car at the price determined at the beginning of the lease. You can turn it in and decide to buy or lease another vehicle. Finally, you can return the vehicle to the dealer and walk away without one. Remember with leasing you can also negotiate the price of the vehicle at the beginning of the contract. Never accept full sticker price.

If leasing is your choice, consider investing a portion of your savings to generate some wealth. The investment returns could help lower your out-of-pocket costs if you decide to purchase the vehicle at the end of the lease or you can use the money for other purposes.

CREDIT CONSIDERATIONS

Just as with renting or buying a home, you will be subject to a credit check if you plan to finance or lease a vehicle. Automobile lenders look at different credit models than mortgage lenders when deciding whether to grant loans. These models take into account all of your credit report, but place more weight on your past car payments. So if you have a checkered history, don't be surprised if the lender charges an annual percentage rate of 20% or more even though current rates may be only 6% for borrowers with "good credit."

Rent to Own

To close out this chapter, we will explore the rent-to-own industry. After you have bought or leased a car and picked a place to live, you will probably want to start shopping for furniture. Some people turn to rent-to-own stores.

More than 8,300 exist nationwide serving 2.7 million customers. But think twice before shopping there. True, they provide a quick way of getting appliances, furniture, consumer electronics and other products. They offer cool incentives to draw you in: No down payments, low weekly or monthly payments without a credit check. If you just need the items for a short period of time such as one month, it may make sense to consider this option. But if your plan is to one day own the item you plan to rent, pass those stores by.

It makes more sense to develop a savings plan and buy the items as you can afford them. Consider this example: The rent to own store offers a television at $12 a week for 78 weeks. At first glance, it may sound affordable. But do the math. That $300 TV will cost you $936 for the convenience of having it now.

Rent to Own versus Cash Sale for a Television

	Payment amount	# of payments	Total cost
Rent to Own	$12	78	$936
Cash sale	$300	1	$300

Before taking the plunge at a rent-to-own store, find out how much it would cost to buy the product outright. The way you do this is to take into account the number of payments needed to purchase the item. Next, there are likely to be handling and delivery charges. The store may also require you to buy insurance to cover the cost of repairs. (Make sure you know who has to pay for repairs because that will increase your costs if you have to bear that burden.)

Once you know all of the costs, add them up and compare that to the price of buying the item outright. Chances are you will pay for the item several times over by using a rent-to-own store. Be sure to read the fine print in the contract because if you get cold feet and want to return the item early, there may be a clause that requires a minimum number of payments before it can be returned. Also be aware that if you miss a payment, the rent-to-own store will take the product back immediately and probably charge you a collection fee.

> ### *Here are some alternatives to using rent-to-own stores:*
>
> - Develop a savings plan to buy the item outright. This is a good option because it doesn't involve using credit.
>
> - Check the Web. Some companies have "Internet only" prices that are lower than buying the item in a physical store.
>
> - Consider used items in excellent condition. You can look around thrift stores or garage sales for your item and possibly negotiate a good price.

NOTES

Just for Teens

Buying your first car

1 My first car was an AB car. It got me from point A to point B. It was a 1978 Buick Regal, which I bought in 1989 for $1,000 before starting my senior year in high school. It was old, but reliable. Buying my own car gave me a feeling of pride. Knowing that I paid for it in full with money I earned made me take good care of it.

2 The benefit of paying cash for a purchase is that it gives you negotiating leverage. The owner might agree to a lower price because he knows he will get the money immediately. Also, by making one lump sum payment, you don't have to worry about monthly statements so you have extra money in your pocket to pay for car insurance and maintenance costs (oil changes and tune-ups).

3 You can find used cars through referrals from sources such as friends or family, classified ads, the Internet, auctions and car dealers. If you can get a referral, that can be a plus because you have someone who can vouch for the character of the vehicle's owner.

4 Watch out for lemons, cars that may look good and start the first time your turn the key, but have hidden problems. Some states have laws offering protection against people selling these defective vehicles. But you can protect yourself by having a mechanic check out the car you're thinking about buying.

5 Another safeguard is to order a vehicle history report. You can purchase one from Carfax.com. It will let you know whether the car has been serviced for repairs related to collision, flood and fire damage.

> *Paying $25 for this report can potentially save you the heartache of spending thousands of dollars in major repairs.*

Shortcuts

- ✓ Renting a place to live often has lower upfront costs than buying a house. Also, you have low to no maintenance costs and usually cheaper monthly payments.

- ✓ Buying a house has lots of benefits, which include some tax breaks. Real estate prices have historically risen 5% per year so you also increase your net worth if you choose to purchase.

- ✓ Leasing a car makes sense if you want to always have a late-model car with low payments and low upfront costs. But if you drive more than 15,000 miles a year, buying may be better because you will not be subject to additional charges for exceeding the mileage allowance.

- ✓ Financing a car over a lengthy term (such as 7 to 8 years) can make you end up with negative equity because the value of vehicles declines rapidly. If you choose to finance your vehicle, try to do it for four years or less.

- ✓ Purchasing from rent-to-own stores gives you the convenience of low weekly payments for big-ticket items such as furniture and electronics. But consider the downside: You can pay for products several times over because of the high interest rates and fees.

CHAPTER 11

≫Investment Basics

A person acquires wealth by buying assets that appreciate over time, such as real estate, stocks and bonds. Their values may go down for a short while, but usually rise over the long haul.

When I was in college I dreamed of owning a Bentley one day, but after I graduated with loads of debt, that thought went out the window. Today, I still think owning a luxury vehicle is nice, but building wealth is even better. Over time, the value of a car will decline. If you invest well, however, your money will grow – and help provide a comfortable retirement life.

Here's the goal: Have your money work for you instead of working for your money. We work hard every day to earn a paycheck to provide for our families and ourselves, but it's even better when the investments we make generate enough income to cover our expenses and allow us to save. This allows us to work because we want to — not because it's a necessity.

Types of Investments

STOCKS

Holding a stock means having ownership in a company. The more shares you own, the bigger stake you have in the firm. Every time it makes money, you earn profits as a shareholder.

The flip side is also true. If the company loses money and decreases in value or goes bankrupt, you will also lose money. Stocks are considered risky investments because they can go up or down on any given day. But in the long run, you will benefit from owning stock in a company that is making profits. Your investment could lead to a higher stock price and dividends, which are company earnings that are paid to shareholders.

Stocks are like people. They go through different "phases." A stock's journey begins with an initial public offering (IPO). This is when a company offers stock to the public for the first time. After this phase, stocks go through a growth spurt. Companies are usually small- to mid-sized when they go through this period of producing sales and earnings that increase at a brisk pace. Also during this stage, profits are often reinvested into the company to fund future opportunities.

After the growth phase, stocks reach maturity. At this point, the company is usually large and has more consistent and stable profits than growth companies, whose earnings can fluctuate drastically.

These mature companies are sometimes referred to as "blue chip" stocks. In poker, the blue chips have the most value, and the same holds true for stocks. Blue chip companies are household names. You've heard them: Wal-Mart, McDonald's, Microsoft. These are companies that have been around for several years and are considered safer investments because they have built a strong reputation in the marketplace. In general, blue chip companies are more likely to pay dividends than smaller and mid-sized ones.

The last group of stocks is known as "penny stocks." Definitions differ as to what price a company must reach to become a penny stock. Some say that if the price is below $5, that constitutes a penny stock. Others suggest prices below $1 should be considered penny stocks.

These stocks are considered risky, because the companies offering them are small with little or no operating history. Many firms will send e-mails to encourage the purchase of penny stocks. If the stock price is below $1, it is best to avoid buying it because there is a chance it will go out of business, causing you to lose your investment.

More on Penny Stocks

If you're regularly online, you may have received an e-mail claiming to have a "hot" stock tip that will bring big returns in a short period of time. It is common for these emails to feature stocks trading at prices less than $5 per share. Beware of these scams. Do your own research on stocks and never just follow a recommendation just because a stockbroker or newsletter is pushing it.

Stock Scam Examples:

Be wary of any e-mails similar to these:

"Happy New Year........

This one could double by the end of the week. Look for increased volume and huge appreciation. This is only the start of a very aggressive campaign.

Watch this one Rock the Year Year!!!"

....

"We feel that this is a move for everyday starting Jan 3, 2006

Market Cap: 1.16M
Current Price: $1.87
Short Term: $5.00

....

As we look for that One Special deal that the public has not come across we Find ABC. We gave it to our Clients one week ago at $1.25 and everyday have watch in amazement as this Company is trading and growing every second. We have no choice but to release this as a Very Special Plat to ALL our clients and say you must watch this first thing Tuesday morning as we see BIG things happening.

WE TELL YOU TO WATCH!!!

STILL NOT TOO LATE!

TRADING ALERT!!!

Timing is everything!!!

Profits of 200-400% EXPECTED TRADING"

....

"For pennies you can participate in a ST0CK that could yield results over and over again just based on the trading patterns if the company is able to effectuate it DKDY'S business model.

WATCH OUT!!!

We could see a GREAT STORY IN THE MAKING."

Analyzing Stocks

There is an old saying that bears repeating here: Invest in what you know. Before buying shares of individual companies, make sure you understand the firm's products and services. I often write a one-page report on the company for my records. It doesn't have to be detailed, but here are some elements it should include:

Description – Give an overview of the company. List the major products or services. You can find this information by visiting the company's Web site or going to Web sites like Yahoo Finance (finance.yahoo.com); CNN Money (money.cnn.com); and MSN Money (moneycentral.msn.com).

Also, take a look at the company's annual report, a public document that companies present to shareholders on a yearly basis. You can request a hard copy of annual reports or view them online.

Strengths – If you plan to invest your money in a company, it should have some positive factors that make it a compelling buy. Maybe it has more market share than other companies in a particular industry, or maybe it has a niche product that is very important to a certain demographic. I recommend finding at least three company strengths before deciding to invest your money.

Weaknesses – Although we often have grand plans when we invest in companies, they don't always work out. That's why it's important to understand the firm's weaknesses. Every company has them, so therefore, no stock is perfect.

Remember this: If a stock you invest in doesn't give you the return you had in mind, you can always look back at the company's weaknesses to determine what went wrong. When choosing a stock, make sure the strengths outweigh the weaknesses. Otherwise, it is probably not a wise investment.

Basic Stock Template

This is an example of a simple one-page report you can put together with just a little time and research:

DESCRIPTION

XYZ Corporation is one of the largest consumer electronic retailers in the Southeast. The company offers installation services for home entertainment and computer-related products. XYZ Corporation is headquartered in Jacksonville, Florida, and has 312 stores in 7 states. Last year, sales were up 25%.

STRENGTHS

Provides great customer service

XYZ Corporation sends it sales staff through a rigorous on-the-job training program in which it stresses that employees are familiar with and understand the products in their department. Employees don't receive commissions for sales, so there is no conflict of interest with the customer.

Low Prices

Management states that it receives volume discounts by ordering in large quantities. Portions of the savings are passed on to customers.

Internet

XYZ has begun selling its products over the Internet. This allows the company to reach customers outside the geographic location of its physical stores and could lead to improved sales in the future.

Weaknesses

Competition

EFG Stores, the largest consumer electronics retailer in the United States, has been opening stores in the Southeast and plans to build stores near XYZ's in an attempt to win over its customers.

Stock Price Movement

Over the past six months, XYZ's stock price has been up by 25%. Although business appears to be going well, it may make more sense to wait for the stock price to come down before buying.

Stock Market Indexes

If you watch business channels such as Bloomberg, CNBC or even the network evening news, you'll hear reporters talk about stock market indices like the S&P 500 or NASDAQ. Below are descriptions of some of the more popular ones:

Dow Jones Industrial Average – This is an index of 30 of the largest publicly-traded companies in the U.S. Some firms in this index include Coca Cola, General Electric, Home Depot, McDonald's and Wal-Mart.

NASDAQ Composite – This index tracks more than 3,000 stocks listed on the NASDAQ Stock Market. Because technology stocks make up a large percentage of this benchmark, some look at it as a proxy for that sector.

S&P 500 – This index is viewed by many investment professionals as a good representation of the U.S. stock market. It consists of 500 companies, which have a broader cross-section of the market than the Dow Jones Industrial Average.

Wilshire 5000 – More than 5,000 stocks are included in this index, making it the broadest measure of stock performance in the U.S.

BONDS

Stocks represent ownership. Bonds represent debt. A bond is a long-term loan issued by a corporation or government agency in order to raise money. That's where your investment comes in.

When you buy a bond, you're lending money. The issuer pays interest on the loan you've given them, typically twice a year. Typically, bonds are distributed in $1,000 and $5,000 denominations. For example, if you buy a bond with a face value of $1,000 that has a 7% interest rate, the corporation or government agency issuing the bond would pay you $70 in interest annually ($1,000 * 7%). And, because interest payments are usually made twice a year, you would receive two checks for $35 each. Upon maturity, (the date the loan must be repaid), you would receive your principal back ($1,000, as in the above example).

U.S. GOVERNMENT BONDS

The U.S. Treasury issues bonds to fund government operations and pay down the national debt. These are backed by the full faith and credit of the U.S. Government; therefore, there is very little chance of default, and these bonds are considered safe investments. But they do have lower interest rates than corporate bonds.

Treasury Inflation Protected Bonds (TIPs)

One of the arguments some investors have against bonds is that they provide minimal returns when you consider inflation. Say the rate of inflation is 3% and your bond is paying 4%. Your real return is only 1% (4% return -3% inflation).

To combat this problem, the U.S. Government created Treasury Inflation Protected Bonds, also known as TIPs. Similar to traditional bonds, holders of TIPs receive interest payments twice a year. However, unlike traditional bonds, where your principal is set for the term, TIPs are adjusted based on the Consumer Price Index (CPI).

The CPI is the most commonly used measure of inflation in the United States. If the economy is in an inflationary environment, the principal will be increased based on the increase of the CPI. If the CPI is declining, (deflationary), the principal balance of your bond will decline. At maturity, you will receive either your original principal balance or adjusted balance, whichever is greater.

Corporate Bonds

Companies issue bonds for a number of reasons: to buy new equipment, build a new facility or finance current operations, for example. Corporate bonds typically pay higher interest than comparable government bonds, but they carry additional risk. If a company goes bankrupt, it may not be able to make interest payments. Although bondholders would receive their money back before stockholders in such an event, there is a chance that you would only receive a fraction of your initial investment or nothing at all. Also, the interest you receive on corporate bonds is taxed.

Municipal Bonds

Municipal bonds are issued by state and local governments to pay for projects such as schools and road repairs. The interest received on these loans is usually exempt from state and local taxes, provided you reside in the state where you bought the bond. The interest rate is lower than a corporate bond with the same maturity, because the interest on a municipal bond is tax-free.

For example, if you have a corporate bond that pays 6% and a municipal bond that pays 5%, to determine which bond is better, you need to add back the tax to the municipal bond.

Here's a simple formula to "do the math": $R/(1-t)$, where R is the interest rate on the municipal bond and t is the tax rate. Assuming you are in the 28% tax bracket and are receiving 5% interest, the formula would look like this: 5%/(1-28%), which equals 6.94%. This is clearly higher than the 6% from the corporate bond, so in this case, the municipal bond is a more attractive investment opportunity when you adjust for taxes.

Bond Quality Ratings

Just as consumers have credit scores, bond issuers receive ratings. The two main bond rating agencies are Standard & Poors and Moody's. They grade companies on their abilities to make interest payments and repay the bond in full at maturity.

For Standard & Poors, the highest rating an issuer can achieve is AAA, while the lowest is CC.

Any bond rated below BBB is considered a "junk" bond. Just as individuals with bad credit have to pay higher interest rates for loans, bond issuers with poor credit ratings have to pay investors a high interest rate for taking on the risk. Junk bonds offer better interest rates than higher quality bonds, but there is a good chance the bond issuer may not be able to pay the interest because it does not have enough cash.

Below is a table with Standard & Poors ratings.

Rating	Description
AAA	Highest rating. Extremely Strong
AA	Very Strong
A	Strong
BBB	Good
BB	Marginal
B	Weak
CCC	Very Weak
CC	Extremely Weak

INTERNATIONAL

It's important to remember although the U.S. market is the largest, almost 50% of the world's stock market value is outside of America. By just focusing on what's offered at home, you may miss out on opportunities to participate in growth around the globe. Emerging markets such as India, China and Brazil are growing more rapidly than the U.S. market.

Investing internationally can enhance returns by giving your portfolio exposure to faster-growing economies and lower risk because the fluctuations can differ from our markets. Just because a certain category of U.S. stocks are going down, for instance, does not mean stocks in other countries are. Although international exposure can increase returns, always remember — it does carry risk.

If you have a mutual fund prospectus and read the fine print, you will see this statement: "Past performance is no indicator of future performance." A particular market having strong returns one year does not guarantee it will continue.

There is also currency risk. If the U.S. dollar goes up in value, it will lower the value of foreign investments you own. This is because when you sell the securities, you will have to convert them back into U.S. dollars, which will be worth less because of the dollar's strength.

One final risk to consider is political unrest. Some countries experience military coups or other types of turmoil, which can negatively influence the stock and bond markets in a particular region. One of the easiest ways to invest overseas is to buy an international mutual fund. Portfolio managers have knowledge of the region, and may actually live there. They can use their skill in constructing a portfolio of stocks that reduces risk for you.

REAL ESTATE

Consider adding real estate investments to your retirement portfolio. There are a number of ways to do this, but one of the easiest is by using real estate investment trusts (REIT). Unlike real estate transactions, in which you buy or sell property using agents, which can cost several thousands of dollars, REIT offers exposure to a portfolio of real estate investments by buying just one share from your stockbroker and paying a minimal commission.

The National Association of Real Estate Investment Trusts Index averaged an annual return of 13.87% from 1995 to 2005, easily outpacing the performance of stocks (9.07% for the S&P 500) and bonds (7.27% for the Lehman Government/Credit Index) over that same time period.

A REIT is a company that invests in real estate directly or buys mortgages. It may invest in shopping malls, hotels, apartments or office buildings. These trusts must pay out at least 90% of earnings in the form of dividends, so they typically offer higher dividends than most stocks and bonds. You also receive a tax benefit with your investment. Corporations must pay taxes on their earnings, and dividends to those who own stock are taxed, so they are subject to double taxation. However, REITs do not pay corporate income tax; therefore, dividends paid to shareholders are tax-free.

Another benefit is that you can buy REITs from your broker, just like you would with any stock or mutual fund, which is faster and less expensive than using a real estate agent.

The final advantage of REITs is liquidity. Because they are listed on the major stock exchanges, all you have to do is place a trade with your stockbroker, and you can sell them that particular day. This is of course in contrast to selling a piece of property, which may take months because it takes time to find a willing buyer.

COMMODITIES

Commodities are products we consume such as coffee, orange juice, meat products (hogs, beef, chicken); or grains (wheat and corn).

Commodities are also items we use, such as precious metal (gold, silver, platinum); and energy (crude oil, natural gas, unleaded gas). During the past two years, we have felt the effects of rising gas prices because of various factors, such as the war with Iraq and hurricanes that damaged oil refineries in the Gulf of Mexico.

In cold weather, we consume more energy, which raises the price of heating oil and natural gas, requiring us to pay more to heat our homes. A few years ago, there was a "Mad Cow" scare, which caused the price of cattle to go up, making it more expensive to buy beef products. We don't often think of commodities as an area to invest for retirement, but we can profit from price increases in the products we use every day.

Most assets, such as stocks and bonds, are hurt by inflation. However, though rising commodity prices are an indication of inflation, you can buy things like gold or oil stocks to actually profit from inflation.

If there is an unexpected increase in inflation, for instance, stock and bond market averages may decline, but commodities may rise because higher prices mean increased demand for the raw materials used in the goods we consume. This protects investors against inflation.

An easy way to invest in commodities is to buy a mutual fund or exchange traded fund, which will be discussed later in this chapter, that invests only in commodities.

Diversified Investment Choices

For investors who lack the time or desire to choose their own stocks and bonds, mutual funds and exchange traded funds, offer a broad exposure to investment choices with low minimum investments.

Mutual Funds

Mutual funds are financial instruments that allow investors to pool their money together. Portfolio managers are responsible for deciding which securities are purchased and sold.

The most common types of mutual funds are stocks, bonds and balanced funds. Balanced funds are a combination of stocks and bonds. Stock funds can be further divided into other classifications, based on the types of securities purchased. Some of these include:

Market Value – Some mutual funds only buy stocks of companies within a specific market value range. You will have mutual funds that may only invest in small, mid-sized, or large companies.

Geographic Location – Mutual funds that invest only in U.S.-based companies or other specific regions of the world.

Style – You may hear the terms "growth fund" or "value fund" from time to time. A growth fund invests in stocks that are expected to increase faster than the average company.

Now, with the prospect of quick growth comes more risk. But remember, the younger you are, the more risks you can afford to take. A 22-year-old, for example, may want to consider having a greater allocation of growth stocks in his or her portfolio than a 65-year-old retiree.

The younger person has several years to make up for any stock market losses, whereas the older person is more likely to depend on more conservative investments for a steady source of income in the form of dividends and interest payments.

Value stocks, on the other hand, produce slower and more stable earnings. They are less volatile and are perceived to be less risky than growth stocks. Value funds also typically have a higher dividend yield, making them an attractive investment choice.

Index – There are several types of indexes that mutual funds can track. There are broad ones, such as the Wilshire 5000 Index, or narrow ones, which follow a specific sector of stocks, like computer-related companies.

For investors who have little desire in outpacing the returns on the major stock market averages and want to pay lower fees, index funds make a lot of sense. Fees on index funds average 0.20% annually versus the average mutual fund, with fees exceeding 1%.

The major benefit of a mutual fund is that you can own a diversified portfolio of securities with a smaller investment than it would cost to purchase several stocks on your own. Some mutual fund "families" will allow you to start with as little as a $500 initial investment.

Mutual Fund Fees

Front end load – This fee is used to pay commissions to a salesperson. It is charged during the first year of owning a mutual fund and can range from 3% to 8.5%.

Back end load – The opposite of a front-end load, this means you pay your sales charge when you sell instead of when you buy. This fee averages 3% and is deducted when you sell your mutual fund shares. If you own the mutual fund for a number of years, usually seven, you won't be charged a back-end load.

Redemption fees – These are charged by some mutual funds to discourage short-term trading. Some investors want to constantly switch between mutual funds, so some firms use redemption fees to discourage this kind of "jumping around." If fund shares are sold within a short period of time (usually one year), the investor may be subject to fees as high as 2%.

12b-1 fees – This covers the cost of advertising and promotions for the fund. By law, this fee cannot be more than 0.75% of your investment.

Management fees – Portfolio managers and their support staff must be paid for their work. As such, they receive the management fee, which averages 0.50% of your investment.

Expense ratio – When you add all of a mutual fund's costs mentioned above, you end up with an expense ratio.

Exchange Traded Funds (ETFs)

Exchange traded funds are baskets of stocks that mirror the portfolio of a particular stock or bond index. It may be a broad one like the Russell 3000, or a more narrow one, such as the Dow Jones Energy Sector.

There are currently more than 150 ETFs offered in the United States. I am a big fan of ETFs because they are an easy way to carry out an asset allocation strategy, which will be discussed in Chapter 12. Here are a few of the benefits of ETFs versus mutual funds:

Transparency – You can go to www.amex.com each day to find out which securities are held in a particular ETF. Mutual funds don't disclose holdings to investors on a daily basis.

Flexibility – ETFs are priced continuously throughout the day, allowing you to buy or sell at specific prices, like you would for stocks. Mutual funds are priced only once daily, at the end of the day.

Diversification – You get instant diversification by buying just one share of an ETF. For example, one share of the S&P 500 ETF gives you exposure to the 500 stocks in that index.

Some mutual fund companies require minimum deposits of $5,000 or more to open an account. With ETFs, you can buy as many or as few shares as you wish through your stockbroker. They're a great way to start investing if you don't have a lot of money.

For more information check on exchange traded funds, check out www.amex.com.

NOTES

Just for Teens

1 One of the best ways to learn more about stocks is to pick a couple of companies and do some simple research. If a firm you choose has several retail stores, for example, you can visit one of its locations to make observations. You can also find information by visiting the company's Web site. Most have an "investor relations" section, which gives information about products and services in an easy-to-understand style.

Also, check out Web sites like Yahoo Finance (finance.yahoo.com) and MSN Money (moneycentral.msn.com) for stock quotes, price charts and company news.

2 After you have done your research, write a brief report that includes a description of the company, along with some positives and a few weaknesses (Refer to sample template on pages 146-147.)

3 Going through this process will give you a first-hand look into how investment professionals analyze firms. It will also give you a better understanding of how the company operates so you can decide whether it is a good investment or not.

4 If, after your analysis you decide to invest, you can ask your parents or a guardian to set up a custodial account with Sharebuilder (www.sharebuilder.com). Custodial accounts are set up by adults to benefit minors. Then, once you reach the age your state considers you to be an adult, you gain full control of the account. Sharebuilder allows you to buy as few shares as you wish and does not require you to have a minimum amount to open your account. You will, however, have to pay a commission to Sharebuilder each time you buy or sell a stock.

Shortcuts

- ☑ Owning a share of stock represents ownership in a company. If you decide to buy an individual stock on your own, do your homework and make sure you understand what you're getting.

- ☑ When corporations or government agencies want to borrow money, they issue bonds. Most bonds pay interest on a semi-annual basis. U.S. Treasuries are among the safest bonds to invest in because they are backed by the full faith and credit of the federal government, whereas corporate bonds are more risky because a corporation may go bankrupt and not be able to repay its bondholders.

- ☑ With mutual funds and exchange traded funds, you have the opportunity to build a diversified portfolio for much less than you would pay by purchasing individual stocks and bonds on your own.

- ☑ Real estate investment trusts are like mutual funds because they are a collection of investments, but they invest solely in real estate. This is a low-cost way of buying and selling real estate because transactions can be completed by placing a trade with your stockbroker as opposed to going through a real estate agent, which can take months to complete.

- ☑ Commodities are raw materials used to produce a lot of products we find in our everyday life such as coffee, orange juice or gasoline. Investing in these assets is a good way to protect yourself against the effects of inflation. Increased demand for goods will lead to higher commodity prices, which in turn leads to higher prices for the products we use.

CHAPTER 12

> ≫ Retirement Planning

Starting retirement planning early in your career does not guarantee success, but it puts time on your side. That can raise your odds of achieving financial freedom so you can enjoy your golden years.

According to a 2003 report by the National Center for Health Statistics, the average American will live to age 78. Who wants to live paycheck-to-paycheck when they're elderly? You can claim a different financial future right now by saving while you are young.

Here are a few accounts where you can consider socking away funds for your retirement:

Brokerage Accounts

When you buy or sell publicly-traded stocks or bonds, you usually do so through a brokerage firm. Full-service brokers provide benefits such as company research to help you choose your investments wisely. This is convenient if you have no time to do the homework yourself or are relatively new to investing.

Brokers also offer products and services like insurance and estate planning. Commissions at some firms can start at $50 per trade.

Discount brokers, on the other hand, offer lower commissions to perform your investment transactions (I've seen commissions as low as $5 per trade), but have fewer services. It's a no-frills way to invest. If you do your own research on the investments you buy, a discount broker may be the way to go because you will save a lot of money.

Retirement Accounts

IRAs

"IRA" stands for Individual Retirement Account. These accounts allow you to save for retirement and receive a tax benefit.

There are two basic types of IRAs: Roth and Traditional. Both are good savings options for employees of companies without other types of retirement vehicles (401(k) or pension plans) or for those who want to save above and beyond contributions to company-sponsored plans.

Roth IRAs

Your earnings will grow tax-free in a Roth IRA, but contributions are made with after-tax dollars. To participate, your income has to fall below certain limits. In 2005, it was $110,000 for singles and $160,000 for married couples. If your income exceeds that amount, you can contribute to a non-deductible IRA, but not a Roth IRA. Withdrawals made after you reach age 59 ½ are tax-free. Also, if your account has been open for at least five years, you can withdraw earnings and contributions without a penalty.

Traditional IRAs

Traditional IRAs will give you a tax break today (provided your income doesn't exceed limits — $60,000 for singles and $80,000 for couples in 2005), but you will have to pay taxes on withdrawals at your current income tax rate.

That's not necessarily a big deal. You may be in the 33% tax bracket while you are working full time, but in retirement you could potentially fall to the 15% tax bracket (assuming your income drops). So, although you will owe taxes, you won't have to pay as much in retirement.

These accounts were designed for retirement purposes, so there are penalties if you make withdrawals before age 59½. There are certain exceptions for situations such as buying your first home, paying medical expenses or death.

IRA Summary

One thing to remember when you set up an IRA is that although traditional IRAs can be converted to Roth IRAs, a Roth IRA cannot be switched back to a traditional IRA. Just make sure you think carefully before opening up a Roth IRA.

If your income exceeds the annual limit for traditional IRA, a Roth IRA makes sense because at least your earnings grow tax-free even though your contributions are not tax-deductible.

Deciding which type of IRA to open basically comes down to whether you want to pay taxes on your retirement money now or in the future.

Whether you choose a Roth or traditional IRA, you have more flexibility than you would with a 401(k) plan when choosing your investments. 401(k) plans typically offer a limited number of mutual funds to select from, whereas you have wide variety of options such as individuals stocks, bonds and mutual funds to choose from with an IRA.

Traditional versus Roth IRAs

	Traditional	Roth
Tax-free withdrawals	No	Yes
Tax-deductible contributions	Yes*	No
Tax-deferred growth	Yes	No

* Subject to income limits

DEFINED BENEFIT/PENSION PLANS

A pension will pay you a fixed amount each month after you retire. These plans are sometimes referred to as "defined benefit programs," because you know in advance what you will be receiving.

Companies that offer these plans have different ways of calculating how much you will be paid. Some base your pension on how many years you've worked at the company, while others base it on a percentage of your salary.

Employees are not required to contribute to these plans because employers assume the responsibility and also make investment choices on their behalf. It's great if you can find a company that is offering a pension, because they are becoming a thing of the past. More and more companies and government organizations are shifting the burden to employees by switching to 401(k) plans. Some companies make the change because people are living longer today than they did in the past.

Firms with pension plans make assumptions on the returns they need from investments in order to meet their obligations and pay benefits to retirees. During the first three years of this century, United States stock market returns were negative, which means it is costing companies more to maintain these plans because their stock market projections were too optimistic.

401(K)/403(B) PLANS

401(k) and 403(b) plans are personal retirement plans for employees. 401(k) plans are offered to workers at most large companies as well as smaller ones. 403(b) programs are offered to employees at educational institutions and some non-profit organizations. Both plans are similar, so the discussion that follows will focus on 401(k) programs. With 401(k) plans, companies may match your contributions up to a certain percentage, but ultimately it is up to you to make investment choices. Just as companies with defined benefit plans make assumptions about various factors affecting pensions, you will have to determine how much you will need in retirement.

There are tools on the Internet that can assist you, such as calculators on Bank Rate (http://www.bankrate.com/brm/calc/.asp), or Banksite.com (http://www.banksite.com/calc/annuity2). On these sites, you will have to input how much of a return you expect each year. I suggest using a number between 7% and 10%. Though you may earn more from your investments, this will give you a reasonable estimate.

Once you determine the amount you need to achieve your goal, you can develop a savings plan. You should contribute as much as possible to your 401(k), because your contributions are completely tax-deductible — up to $15,000. (That figure is as of this printing.)

Also, by participating in these plans you have the opportunity to get "free money" if your employer matches your deposits. Your contributions "vest" immediately, which means that if you decide to leave the company, you will still own 100% of your contributions and earnings. Company contributions may vest over a period of years.

Vesting

The three types of vesting are immediate, graded, and cliff.

Immediate – All of your contributions vest as soon as you sign up. Some companies also have retirement plans in which its contributions become yours as soon as you become a participant in the plan.

Graded Vesting (Graduated) – With this type of plan, you earn a portion of your employer's contributions each year. Let's say it will take you five years before you're fully vested. That means in your first year, you own 20% of your employer's contributions. In the second year, you own 40%. It continues each year at that rate until year five, when you own all contributions made by your company.

Cliff Vesting – With cliff vesting, you own all contributions after you have been on the job for a certain number of years. For example, if the company uses a period of three years, you would own all contributions made by your company after year three. If you leave during your second year, you would receive all of your deposits, but none of employer's.

Start Early

If your company offers a 401(k) plan, I heartily encourage you to participate. Even if you can only contribute 1% of your salary, it will make a difference over time. The chart below shows the benefits of starting your investment plan early.

The chart below reflects an annual salary of $24,000 with a 3% employee contribution and a 3% matching employer contribution. I also assumed a 9% annual return on your investments. If you plan to retire in 40 years, your balance would accumulate to more than $560,000 by investing just $60 per month from you and an additional $60 from your company.

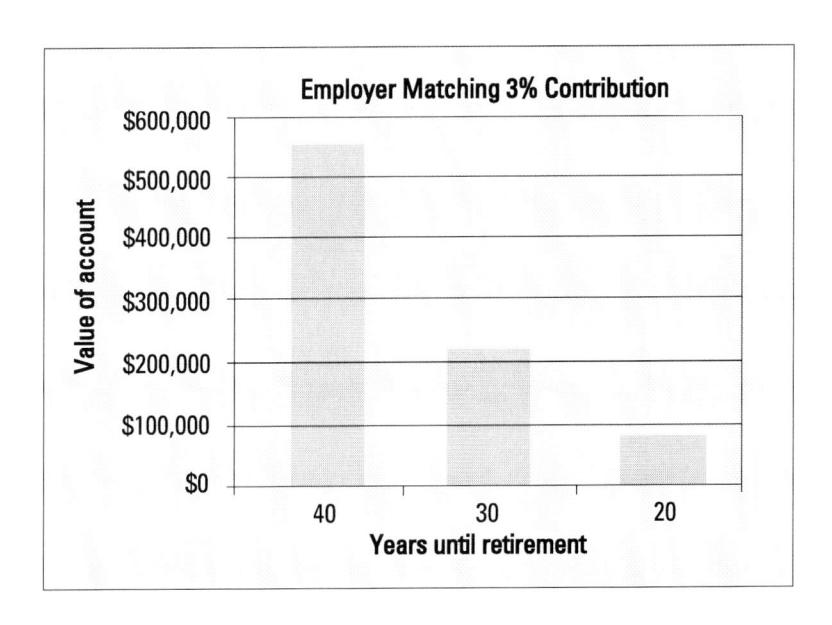

| To become a millionaire by age 65 invest: ||
Age	Monthly Investment*
16	$94
18	$113
20	$135
30	$340
40	$892
50	$2,643

*Assumes 9% annual returns

Again, the earlier you start saving, the less money you will need overall to meet your goals. The example on the previous page for instance, only requires you to contribute $60 per month. This way, you can prepare for retirement without sacrificing your lifestyle.

Withdrawals

Though there is a 10% penalty for withdrawals made before you reach 59 ½, certain withdrawals are allowed without penalty for the following reasons:

- Buying a home;
- Paying medical expenses for yourself or dependents;
- Funding certain post-secondary educational expenses;
- Preventing eviction or foreclosure from your primary home.

Also, if you're really strapped for cash, you can take out loans from your 401(k) account. Some suggest this is a good way to get cash for emergencies. I discourage it unless it is a last resort, because these loans must be repaid with interest. The good part is that you are essentially paying yourself back with interest. The downside is that if you leave the company before you repay the loan, the balance is due immediately. If you don't have the funds at that time to repay it, your loan is treated as a withdrawal, which is subject to tax penalties.

Rollovers

When you change jobs, there are three options available for your 401(k) account: (1) Leave it with your former employer's plan; (2) Roll it into an IRA or another 401(k) plan; (3) Cash it out. Note, however, that cashing out your plan before reaching age 59 ½ subjects you to early withdrawal penalties.

Putting It All Together

When you create your retirement plan, strive to construct a diversified portfolio consisting of stocks, bonds, commodities and real estate. Stocks and bonds are traditionally the easiest to invest in, but with the introduction of exchange traded funds and some new mutual funds, real estate and commodities are now available to the average investor.

The benefits of having these assets is they do not perform entirely like stocks or bonds, thereby lowering your overall risk while potentially boosting returns.

As far as stocks go, consider U.S. and international stocks. The latter pose a greater risk because certain countries have unstable governments and the markets are less established. But the return potential can be greater because there are leading companies in several industries based outside the U.S. that are growing faster than ones headquartered here. The performance of international stocks, like commodities and real estate, is not connected to U.S. stock price movements.

Asset Allocation

Asset allocation is the process of dividing your investment funds between the major asset classes (stocks, bonds, real estate, commodities, etc.) to get the highest return and manage risk.

Some refer to asset allocation as not "putting all of your eggs in one basket." The younger you are, the more risk you can afford to take. So, a 21-year-old should own a bigger percentage of risky investments, such as growth and international stocks, than someone nearing retirement age.

Why is Asset Allocation Important?

Studies have shown that asset allocation accounts for a majority of investment returns. Therefore, picking the right stock isn't as important as having broad exposure to several asset classes (e.g., stocks, bonds, real estate and commodities).

Because the performance of each group isn't dependent on the other, it reduces risk. Let's say the prices of stocks are going down in the face of weak economic news: bond, commodity, and real estate prices may rise because they are driven by totally different factors. With asset allocation, your whole investment doesn't suffer if one asset class tanks, because you have exposure to other groups that may be going up while others are declining.

Many investors focus only on the stock market and miss out on opportunities in other investment groups. You may own a stock mutual fund, for instance, and decide to sell because stock prices are falling. But meanwhile, commodity prices or bonds may have been rising. You would miss out on that opportunity because your money was sitting in cash, generating minimal returns.

Don't wait until the timing is "just right" for you to invest. If you start early and use a disciplined strategy, you will make money in the long run. So let your money work for you by investing it in vehicles like stocks, bonds, real estate, commodities, etc., that have historically increased in value.

John Shedd, an author, once said, "A ship is safe in harbor, but that's not what they are made for." Parking your money in checking and money market accounts will not generate much of an investment return. You have to be willing to take some risks if you want to create a sturdy nest egg for retirement.

How To Implement Asset Allocation

If you search the Internet, you can find tons of advice regarding what percentage of stocks and bonds to own. One popular school of thought is to have 60% of your portfolio in stocks and 40% in bonds. The problem with this strategy is that you miss out on real estate and commodities. Also, it's static: The plan does not adjust based on your age or risk tolerance. You should have a dynamic plan that responds to these variables.

Here's one to consider: Begin determining how to allocate your money by thinking about your age. This number is the amount you should invest in bonds. If you are 20, for example, you would designate 20% of your portfolio to bonds. As you get older, the bond portion of your portfolio will increase because you will want a more stable source of income. A 75-year-old is more concerned about receiving the interest payment checks from bonds than getting growth out of stocks, for example.

Treasury Inflation Protected Securities (TIPs) are a great idea for the bond portion of your portfolio because they protect you in the event of inflation. Although they can decline in a deflationary environment (falling prices), you will never receive less than you initially invested.

Next, designate 10% to 15% of your portfolio to real estate and commodities. These asset classes help reduce risk because their movements aren't tied to stock or bond prices.

The remaining amount of your portfolio should be invested in stocks. While you are young and have several years until retirement, it's a good idea to have the majority of your stock portion invested in small- and mid-sized growth companies because you have time on your side and can make up for any losses that come with owning these riskier stocks over time.

Also, consider having at least 10% of your stock exposure earmarked for international stocks. As mentioned earlier, there are several global stock markets, and owning an international mutual fund can potentially increase returns of your overall portfolio.

Once you determine your asset allocation levels, stick with your plan. Portfolios should be reviewed at least quarterly. Try not to do too much buying and selling in a short period of time because it is important to give your investments time to grow.

With asset allocation, you are reducing the risk that a particular category crashes and burns by spreading your money among asset classes. You may want to hire a professional to help in setting up your strategy because your financial future depends on the decisions you make today.

Questions to Ask a Financial Advisor:

1. *How are you compensated?* Find an advisor who is not paid on commission, because it reduces the conflict of interest between how they are paid and what they recommend. Some financial planners will only sell products from specific companies because they receive commissions from them.

2. *How much experience do you have?* Just as companies ask about your work experience when you are interviewing for a new job, you should find out how long the financial planner has been in the business.

3. *What services do you offer?* Some financial planners specialize in niche products like tax planning. However, you may need one that offers a broad range of insurance and retirement planning products so that as your needs change, you have an advisor who can grow with you.

4. *Can you provide references?* When you check their references, ask what each person likes and dislikes about the planner. Find out how long he or she has been a client and if they are satisfied.

5. *Can I have a written contract?* After you decide on a planner, make sure you get a written contract outlining the services offered and the charges. Keep a copy for future reference.

Just for Teens

Making it a habit of saving while you are young can help you build wealth and may allow you to retire at a young age. Below is a chart showing how much a monthly investment of $25 will grow if you start saving at different ages. The chart reflects how much you would have at age 60, assuming you will earn 9% per year on your investments. In the scenario below, a 16-year-old would have almost $169,000 by age 60. That's just by investing $25 per month.

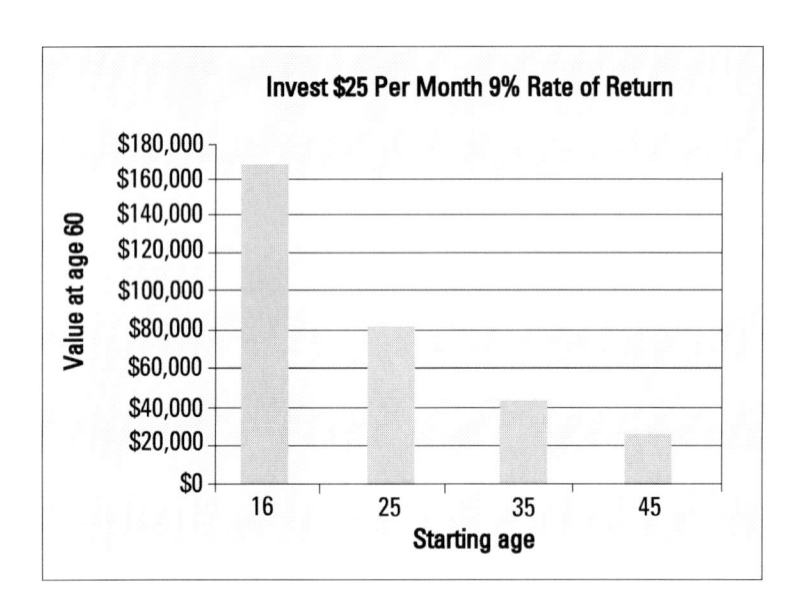

Invest $25 Per Month 9% Rate of Return

Starting age	Value at age 60
16	~$169,000
25	~$82,000
35	~$45,000
45	~$25,000

2 You get the message: The earlier you start saving, the more quickly you build wealth. The stock and bond markets will go up some years and down others, but over time they've historically performed well. So develop a savings plan and stick with it — even during tough times.

> *Time is on your side. If you have a regular source of income, it makes sense to start saving now.*

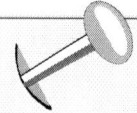

Shortcuts

- [x] IRAs are personal retirement accounts you can set up on your own.

- [x] The two main types of IRAs are Roth and Traditional. Contributions to Roth IRAs are not tax deductible, but your earnings grow tax-free. Traditional IRAs, on the other hand, allow for tax-deductible contributions, provided your income is below the level set by the IRS.

- [x] If your company has a retirement savings plan such as a 401(k), participate if you are eligible. It is a great way of saving for the future. You get "free money" if your employer matches your contribution.

- [x] Asset allocation means you spread your investment funds among different asset classes (e.g., stocks, bonds, real estate, commodities) to reduce your risk and increase your returns.

epilogue

Back when I struggled with credit, I hated to hear the phone ring. I knew it might be collection agencies calling about past-due bills. I remember spending hours at a car dealership hoping the finance manager would find a lender willing to take a chance on me. I didn't have a map to guide my financial decisions. You do.

I hope you will take away from this book a better sense of how to avoid pitfalls, rebound from money problems and claim a successful financial future. I will never forget how good it felt the day I went to purchase a new car and walked into the dealership with a pre-approved loan from my bank. I completed the whole transaction on my lunch break. I knew I was on the path to financial freedom.

Now that you are armed with the tools to succeed, put them to use. You may take some wrong turns along the way, but I hope you've learned how to get back on track and avoid making the same mistakes again.

Thank you for reading my book. I would love to hear from you. Tell me what you enjoyed and what I can improve. Email me at info@PatrickALyons.com or write letters to the address below.

Lyons Den Press
PO Box 1341
Durham, North Carolina 27702

about the author

Patrick Lyons has more than a decade of experience as an investment professional. Currently a portfolio manager at NCM Capital Management Group, Inc., Lyons earned a B.S. in Mathematics from Florida A&M University and an M.S. in Management (Finance Concentration) from North Carolina State University. His investment advice has been featured in Black Enterprise magazine and on Bloomberg Radio. He serves as the stocks editor for msfinancialsavvy.com. Lyons has also taught business finance at Wake Technical Community College and conducted workshops on personal finance for several schools and organizations.

resources

Banking

Federal Deposit Insurance Corporation
1776 F St, N.W.
Washington, DC. 20006
877-275-3342
Supervises banks and insures deposits in these institutions up to $100,000
http://www.fdic.gov/index.html

National Credit Union Administration
1775 Duke St.
Alexandria, VA. 22314-3428
703-518-6300
Supervises credit unions and insures deposits up to $100,000
http://www.ncua.gov/index.html

Credit

AllCardsConsidered.Com
PO Box 184
Sun City, CA. 92585
Educational information on credit cards.
http://www.allcardsconsidered.com

Federal Reserve Board
20th Street and Constitution Avenue, N.W.
Washington, DC. 20551
This link provides useful tips on shopping for a credit card
http://www.federalreserve.gov/pubs/shop/

Equifax
PO Box 740241
Atlanta, GA. 30374
800-685-1111
http://www.equifax.com/

Experian
PO Box 2104
Allen, TX 75013-2104
888-397-3742
http://www.experian.com/

Trans Union
PO Box 2000
Chester, PA. 19022
800-888-4213
http://www.transunion.com/index.jsp

FICO Score estimate
http://www.bankrate.com/brm/fico/calc.asp

National Score Index
Provides national and regional averages of credit scores.
http://www.nationalscoreindex.com/NSI_Site/

AnnualCreditReport.com
PO Box 105283
Atlanta, GA. 30348-5283
877-322-8228
Centralized source for obtaining credit reports from the 3 major credit bureaus.
http://www.annualcreditreport.com

National Foundation for Credit Counseling
801 Roeder Rd.
Suite 900
Silver Spring, MD. 20910
301-589-5600
Information on credit counseling
http://www.nfcc.org/

Credit Repair Organizations Act of 1996
Details laws governing Credit Repair firms
http://www.ftc.gov/os/statutes/croa/croa.htm

Fair Credit Reporting Act
Information on the laws protecting consumers
http://www.ftc.gov/os/statutes/fcrajump.htm

Fair and Accurate Transactions Act of 2003
Added new sections to the Fair Credit Reporting Act to help consumers fight identity theft
http://frwebgate.access.gpo.gov/cgi-bin/getdoc.cgi?dbname=108_cong_public_laws&docid=f:publ159.108.pdf

Center for Responsible Lending
302 West Main St.
Durham, NC 27701
919-313-8500
Organization working to put an end to predatory lending practices
http://www.responsiblelending.org/

Identity Theft

Verified by Visa
Provides information on its program to protect consumers buying products on the Internet
https://usa.visa.com/personal/security/vbv/

National Do Not Call Registry
Attn: DNC Program Manager
Federal Trade Commission
600 Pennsylvania Ave, N.W.
Washington, DC. 20580
Add your home and cell phone to this list to limit telemarketer calls
888-382-1222
https://www.donotcall.gov/default.aspx

Identity Theft Clearinghouse
Federal Trade Commission
600 Pennsylvania Ave, N.W.
Washington, DC. 20580
877-438-4338
Information to educate consumers about identity theft
http://www.consumer.gov/idtheft/

Identity Theft Resource Center
PO Box 26833
San Diego, CA. 92196
858-693-7935
Nonprofit organization focusing exclusively on identity theft
http://www.idtheftcenter.org/alerts.shtml

Phishing e-mails
Anti-Phishing Working Group
http://www.antiphishing.org/index.html

Hoax-Slayer
http://www.hoax-slayer.com/

Job Information

PERSONALITY TESTS
Keirsey Temperament Sorter II
http://www.keirsey.com/

Jung-Myers Briggs
http://www.humanmetrics.com/

JOB WEB SITES
Monster.com
5 Clock Tower Pl, #500
Maynard, MA 01754
888-666-7837
http://www.monster.com

Careerbuilder.com
200 N. Lasalle St
Suite 1100
Chicago, IL. 60601
800-891-8880
http://careerbuilder.com

Yahoo Hotjobs
45 W. 18th St
6th Floor
New York, NY. 10011
646-351-5300
http://hotjobs.yahoo.com/

Internship Opportunities

MonsterTrak
11845 West Olympic Blvd.
Suite 500
Los Angeles, CA. 90064
http://www.monstertrak.com

INROADS, Inc
10 South Broadway
Suite 300
St. Louis, MO. 63102
314-241-7488
http://www.inroads.com

InternWeb
http://www.internweb.com

Entrepreneur

SCORE
409 3rd St, S.W.
6th Floor
Washington, DC 20024
800-634-0245
http://www.score.org/

Entrepreneurs' Organization
500 Montgomery St
Suite 500
Alexandria, VA 22314 USA
703-519-6700
http://www.eonetwork.org

Education

The College Board
Source for information on preparing for college
45 Columbus Ave
New York, NY 10023-6992
(212) 713-8000
http://www.collegeboard.com

Diploma Mills
Information on how to spot diploma mills
http://www.elearners.com/resources/diploma-mills.asp

Council for Higher Education Accreditation
One Dupont Cir, N.W.
Suite 510
Washington, DC. 20036
202-955-6126
List of accredited online programs by state
http://www.chea.org/degreemills/frmStates.htm

National Endowment for Financial Education
5299 DTC Blvd
Suite 1300
Greenwood Village, CO. 80111
303-741-6333
Non-profit that has programs designed to teach consumers about personal finance
http://www.nefe.org/index2.html

JumpStart Coalition for Personal Financial Literacy
919 18th St, N.W.
Suite 300
Washington, DC. 20006
202-466-8604
Seeks to improve financial literacy of young adults
http://www.jumpstart.org/index.cfm

Junior Achievement
One Education Way
Colorado Springs, CO. 80906
800-843-6395

Educates students in grades K-12 about opportunities available in the business world

http://www.ja.org/

Housing/Car Buying

U.S. Department of Housing and Urban Development
451 7th St., S.W.
Washington, DC. 20410
(202) 708-1112
Useful home buying tips
http://www.hud.gov/buying/index.cfm#programs

Fannie Mae
3900 Wisconsin Ave, N.W.
Washington, DC. 20016-2892
800-732-6643
Offers financial products to make housing affordable for low to middle income families
www.fanniemae.com

Carfax.com
Provides vehicle history reports that cover collision, fire, and flood damage
http://www.carfax.com

Edmunds.com
Comprehensive source for on buying new or used vehicles as well as leasing.
http://www.edmunds.com

Kelley Blue Book

195 Technology

Irvine, CA. 92618

800-258-3266

Find the estimated wholesale and retail value of your vehicle

http://www.kbb.com

LemonLawOffice.com

Provides lemon law information for each of the 50 states and a list of lawyers who represent clients who are victims

http://www.lemonlawoffice.com/

HomeGain

1250 45th St.

Suite 200

Emeryville, CA. 94608

888-542-0800

Website helps buyers and sellers find real estate agents

http://www.homegain.com

Investing

Sharebuilder

1445 – 120th Ave, N.E.

Bellevue, WA. 98005

866-747-2537

Allows investors to buy stocks with no minimum account size.

http://www.sharebuilder.com

American Stock Exchange
86 Trinity Pl.
New York, NY. 10006
800-843-2639
Information on Exchange Traded Funds
http://www.amex.com

MUTUAL FUND INFORMATION

Morningstar
225 W. Wacker Dr.
Chicago, IL. 60606
312-696-6000
http://www.morningstar.com

Lipper
3 Times Sq
New York, NY. 10036
877-955-4773
http://www.lipperweb.com

RETIREMENT CALCULATORS

Bankrate.com
11760 US HWY 1
Suite 500
North Palm Beach, FL.33408
561-630-2400
http://www.bankrate.com/brm/calc/401k.asp

Banksite.com
http://www.banksite.com/calc/annuity2

PERSONAL FINANCE WEB SITES

Yahoo Finance
http://finance.yahoo.com

MSN Money Central
http://moneycentral.msn.com

Taxes

Internal Revenue Service
500 N. Capitol St., N.W.
Washington, DC. 20221
800-829-1040
Provides comprehensive source for tax information
http://www.irs.gov/individuals/index.html

index

401(K)/403(B) plans. 96, 162, 164–169, 176
See also Retirement.

A

Accounts, 15, 25–28, 32, 54–57, 61, 74, 161–165, 171, 176
  See also Banking
    brokerage, 26, 95, 161
    checking, 15, 24–31, 42, 47, 171
    money market, 15, 25, 171
    online, 26, 27, 29–31
    retirement, 161–166
    savings, 25–26
Apartments, 64, 69, 123
    benefits of, 123, 124, 126
    insurance, 124
    maintenance costs, 126, 140
    monthly expenses, 10, 12–13, 15–16, 124
    move-in costs, 124
    rental, 123–124
    roommates, 10, 19
Asset allocation, 157, 170–173, 177
Auto leasing, 123, 134–136
Auto purchase, 134
    credit for, 136
    financing of, 136
    negotiating, 134–135, 139
Auto title loans, 48–49, 52

B

Back end load, 156–157. *See also* Mutual Funds
Banking, 23–32
    accounts, 24
    ATM fees, 24, 29–30
    bill pay, 27
    brokerage, 26
    charges, 28
    checking, 25, 31
    check fees, 28–29
    choosing an institution, 23–25, 30
    direct deposit, 30
    insufficient funds, 28
    minimum balance fees, 29
    money market accounts, 25
    online, 26–27
    savings, 26
    stop payments, 29
    virtual, 28–30
    wire transfers, 29
Bankruptcy, 14, 54, 64, 66
    law, 67–68
    types of, 54, 66–67
Banks vs. credit unions, 23–32
Bond quality ratings, 150
Bonds, 148–151
    corporate, 148–149, 160
    government, 148
    junk bonds, 150
    municipal, 150
    quality ratings, 150
    Treasury Inflation Protected, 149, 172
    Standard & Poors Ratings, 151
Brokerage accounts, 26, 161–162

Budgeting, 9–10, 12–13, 15–16
    clothing costs, 16
    emergencies, 14
    living expenses, 19. *See also* Renting and Home Ownership
    online shopping, 17–18
    samples of, 12, 22
    savings tips, 15
    software for, 13
    splurge fund, 15
    setting up, 17
    transportation costs, 16
    wholesale clubs, 17
Business plans, 101–102, 105, 110
    company overview, 102
    developing, 101
    executive summary, 101
    financial projections, 104
    management, 103
    marketing plan, 102
    milestones, 104
    product overview, 102
    review, 104
Business, starting your own, 99–110

C

Careers, 87–98
    assessment of, 88
    internships, 91
    personality tests, 88
        Jung–Myers–Briggs Typology, 88
        Keirsey Temperament Sorter II, 88
Check cards, 42
Checking accounts, 25. *See also* Banking

Closing costs, 124–125, 128. *See also* Home Purchasing
    appraisal fees, 125
    attorney fees, 125
    credit report fees, 125
    home inspection fees, 125
    origination fees, 125
    points, 125
    Private Mortgage Insurance (PMI), 125
Clothing costs, 16
College education, 113–122. *See also* Education
Commodities, 154
Community college, 115. *See also* Education
Continuing education, 113
Credit, 35
    auto title loans, 48
    bureaus, 56, 59
    charge-offs, 63
    check cards, 42
    collection accounts, 54–56, 64, 69–70
    counselors, 64
    credit cards, 37–42
        choosing, 35–36
        disclosure statement, 38
        interest, 37–41, 46
        secured, 42
        unsecured, 40
    credit lines, 43–44
    credit reports, 53–59
    debit cards, 42
    installment, 43
    minimum payments, 38
    payday loans, 47
    problems, 63
    repair, 64–65
    repair scams, 65–66

    revolving, 37
    scores, 55–56
    service bills, 43
    student loans, 44. *See also* **Student Loans**
        subsidized, 45
        unsubsidized, 45
    types of, 36–38
Credit Repair Organizations Act, 65
Credit reporting agencies, 56, 59
Credit reports, 53–59
    account information, 54
    copies of, 59
    disputes, 58, 71
    inquiries, 54
    personal information, 53
    public records, 54
    scores, 55. *See also* **Credit Scores**
    understanding, 53
    years listed, 54
Credit score, 55–56
    factors influencing, 56
        balance–to–limit, 56
        disputes, 58, 71
        inquiries, 57
        payment history, 56
        types of accounts, 57
Credit unions, 23—32

D

Debit cards, 42
Diploma mills, 119
Disability insurance, 94
Dow Jones Industrial Average, 147

197

E

Education, 113
    community college, 115
    continuing education, 113
    diploma mills, 119
    for adults, 116
    four-year colleges, 116
    hybrid programs, 118
    loans for, 44
    nights & weekend programs, 118
    online, 116–118
    salaries as a result of, 114–115
    student loans, 44
    unemployment, 114–115
Email, 76–83
    chain letters, 79
    hoaxes, 77
    lottery scams, 80
    money laundering, 80
    phishing, 76–79
    diplomas online, 119
    stock scams, 143
Emergency funds, 14
Employment, 87–97
    benefits, 92
        insurance, 93
        paid-time off, 93
        tuition reimbursement, 93
    dream jobs, 87
    finding, 89
        creating a resume, 88
    internships, 91
Entrepreneurs, 99–105
Equifax, 53, 56, 59, 74

Exchange Traded Funds, 155, 157–158, 160, 169
    benefits of, 157–158
Expense worksheets, 10–11
Experian, 53, 56–57, 59, 74

F

Federal Insurance Contributions Act tax (FICA), 96
FICO score, 55–58
Finances, 2, 9–19
    advisors, 173–174
    freedom, 87
    goals, 4–5, 9–10, 87, 101, 168
    institutions, 23, 25, 30, 32, 76
    software programs, 13, 26, 92
Fixed payments, 37, 43, 45, 95, 129
Fraud, 18, 58–59, 73–74
    criminal identity, 74
    email, 76–77
    identity theft, 73
    financial identity, 74
    lottery email, 80
    money laundering, 80
    online, 75
    phishing, 76–79
    types of, 74
Front end load, 156. *See also* Mutual Funds

H

Health insurance, 14, 93–94
Home ownership, 123, 126–127
    benefits of, 126
        fixed rates, 13, 126, 129–130

freedom, 127
net worth, 126
taxes, 126
Home purchasing, 123
application fees, 125
appraisal fee, 125
attorney fees, 125
before you buy, 133
closing costs, 125
credit report fees, 125
credit for 125, 127
home inspection fees, 125
loans, 129
adjustable rate, 129–130
fixed rate, 129–130
interest–only, 130
mortgage brokers, 128
mortgage payments, 131
origination fees, 125
Points, 125
Private Mortgage Insurance (PMI), 125

I

Identity theft, 73
protection from, 73–74, 83
Inflation, 149, 154, 160, 172
Insurance, 93
disability, 94
health, 93–94
life, 94
term life, 95
whole life, 95
Internet education, 116–117
asynchronous, 117

instructors, 117
   life experience, 118
   school accreditation, 117
   synchronous, 117
Internships, 91–92
   sources of, 92
Investing, 141–160
   basics, 141
   bonds, 148
   commodities, 154
   diversify, 155
   Exchange Traded Funds, 155, 157–158, 160, 169
   inflation, 149, 154, 172, 160
   international, 152
   mutual funds, 152–158
   real estate, 153
   stocks, 142–148
IRAs, 162–164

J

Job search, 87–92. *See also* Employment
   company recruitment, 90
   headhunters, 90
   internships, 91–92
   networking, 89
   newspapers, 90
   online, 89, 92
   resumes, 88
   thank you letter, 91
Jung–Myers–Briggs Typology, 88
Just for Teens, 20, 31, 51, 60, 69, 82, 97, 106–108, 121, 139, 159, 175

K

Keirsey Temperament Sorter, 88

L

Leasing, 134–136
Life insurance, 93–95
Loans, 44–52
    auto title, 48–49
    payday, 46–47, 49
    refund anticipation loans, 49
    education, 44

M

Microsoft Money, 13
Money market accounts, 15, 25, 171
Mortgage brokers, 128
Mutual funds, 152–158
    back end load, 156
    balanced funds, 155
    Exchange Traded Funds, (ETFs), 157–158
    fees, 156–158
    front end load, 156
    geographic location, 155
    growth fund, 155
    index, 156
    international, 152
    market value, 155
    style, 155

N

NASDAQ Composite, 147

O

Online banking, 26–27, 29, 32
Online bill pay, 27–28
Online shopping, 17–18, 75

P

Payday loans, 46–47, 49
Penny stocks, 143
Personality tests, 88, 98
Phishing, 76–79
    chain letters, 79
    emails, 76
    hoaxes, 77
    phone, 77

R

Real estate, 126–133, 153
Real Estate Investment Trust Index, 153
Rent vs. buy, 123
Renting apartments, 123
Rent-to-own, 136–137
Rent-to-own stores, 136–138
Resumes, 88. *See also* Job Search
Retirement, 96, 161–176
    401(K)/403(B) plans, 165
    accounts, 162

    IRAs, 162
    IRA summary, 163
    rollovers, 169
    Roth IRAs, 162
    traditional IRAs, 163
    withdrawals, 169
  asset allocation, 170–172
  brokerage accounts, 161–162
  defined benefit plans, 164–165
  pension plans, 164–165
  planning for, 161
  vesting, 166

S

S&P 500, 147
Savings, 21–22, 25–26, 28–29, 42–43, 49, 51–52, 70, 87, 135–136, 138, 162, 165, 175–177
  accounts, 25–26
  clothing costs, 16
  housing costs, 19
  online shopping, 17–18
  retirement, 161–176
  tips, 15–19
  transportation costs, 16–17
  travel costs, 18
  wholesale clubs, 17
Service bills, 43
Service Corps of Retired Executives (SCORE), 104–105
Shortcuts, 21, 32, 52, 61, 70, 83, 98, 110, 122, 140, 160, 176
Software, 13–14
Splurge fund, 15
Standard & Poors rating, 150–151
Starting a business, 99–110
State and local tax, 97

Stocks, 142. *See also* Investing
   analysis of, 145
   descriptions, 145
   indexes, 147
   scams, 143
   strengths of, 145
   templates, 146
   weaknesses of, 145
Student loans, 44–46
   consolidation, 45–46
   interest, 45–46
   repayment, 45
      equal payments, 45
      graduated payments, 45
      income-sensitive, 45
   subsidized, 45
   tips, 46
   unsubsidized, 45

T

Taxes, 96–97
   federal withholding, 96
   FICA, 96
   state and local, 97
Term life insurance, 95
Title loans, 48–49
Transportation costs, 16–17
TransUnion, 56, 59
Travel costs, 18
Travel deals, 18
Treasury Inflation Protected Bonds (TIPs), 149

U

Unemployment rates, 114–115
US government bonds, 148
US Treasury, 148–149

V

Vesting, 166. *See also* Retirement
    cliff vesting, 166
    employer contributions, 167
    graded vesting, 166
    immediate, 166

W

Whole life insurance, 95
Wholesale clubs, 17
Wilshire 5000, 148
Worksheet, for expenses, 11